The **DEFINITIVE** Breed Standard Comparison in **PHOTOS**

Australian Shepherds and Miniature American Shepherds

HELENE NILSEN PHOTOGRAPHY

ANNE FRANÇOISE PHOTOGRAPHY

AKC

FCI

ASCA

ENGLISH 🇬🇧

Paula McDermid • Claudia Bosselmann • Inga Cerbule

"This book is amazing—a wonderful accomplishment! This is a must-have for everyone interested in learning, especially how the word 'moderate' is defined for the Australian Shepherd. A great addition to anyone's library!"

Sheila Polk. Tri-Ivory Australian Shepherds, established in 1963. Founding member of the United States Australian Shepherd Association (USASA). Approved by the American Kennel Club to judge 62 breeds in the Herding, Sporting and Working Groups and Best in Show. Highly respected judge across the U.S.A. and Europe.

"A resource like no other! Our breed has needed this for years. Bravo!"

Tim J. Preston, Cobbercrest Australian Shepherds, established in 1978. Founding member of the United States Australian Shepherd Association (USASA), former USASA President, respected Australian Shepherd breed mentor.

"This book is an accurate and needed comparison of the Australian Shepherd and Miniature American Shepherd Breed standards. It should be read and used as a reference by both judges and breeders."

Sue Ritter. Legacy Australian Shepherds, established in 1980. USASA Hall of Fame breeder of Australian Shepherds, Miniature American Shepherd breeder, judge's educator and mentor, current President of the AKC parent club, Miniature American Shepherd Club USA.

ACKNOWLEDGMENTS

Thank you to the owners and photographers who shared photos of their beautiful dogs, without which this book would have been impossible to create.

Thank you to Bonnie Zuhlsdorf, Dave Birren, and C.A. Sharp for editorial assistance.

Thank you to Claudia Bosselmann, Inga Cerbule, Sheila Polk, Tim Preston, and Sue Ritter for sharing their tremendous knowledge.

First printing May 2002
Updated April 2024

ISBN 978-0-9975534-7-5

Contents

This book illustrates in photos the ideal moderate breed type and characteristics of Australian Shepherds and Miniature American Shepherds according to their breed standards.

How this book is organized

Each section begins with text quoted word-for-word from the breed standards for Australian Shepherds (AUSSIES) followed by the breed standards for Miniature American Shepherds (MAS).

Photographs, diagrams, and supplemental information help clarify the meaning of the breed standards.

Five breed standards are compared

The Australian Shepherd and Miniature American Shepherd breeds have much in common and their breed standards have many similarities. In this book, five breed standards are compared:

- **AKC, FCI and ASCA for Australian Shepherds, and**
- **AKC and FCI for Miniature American Shepherds.**

The ASCA standard was written in 1977 and amended in 2013.
It is the document on which the other standards were based.

The AKC standard for Aussies was approved in 1991 and for Miniature American Shepherds in 2012.

The FCI standard for Aussies was approved in 2009 and for Miniature American Shepherds in 2019.

Importance of breed standards

Breed standards describe the ideal appearance, characteristics, and temperament of a breed. They are a blueprint for a dog who is able to perform the job for which the breed was developed. Breed standards also describe faults that disqualify a dog from reproduction or from being exhibited at conformation shows, and are a guide to discourage the breeding of dogs with conditions or exaggerations that could be detrimental to the health or soundness of the breed.

Reading and understanding a breed standard requires knowledge of specific terminology and dog anatomy, as well as familiarity with the breed overall. The purpose of this book is to fill in knowledge gaps, using photos of correct dogs, and to explain the reasons why traits are desirable or undesirable, according to the breed standards.

Value of conformation shows

A conformation dog show is not a comparison of one dog to another. It is a comparison of **each dog to the breed standard.** The purpose of conformation dog shows is to **evaluate breeding stock.** Judges are expected to select winners based on how closely they meet the breed standard.

Breed fanciers attend conformation shows to exhibit the qualities of their dogs to judges whom they respect, to compete with other breed fanciers, to scout for compatible breeding stock, and to enjoy friendships with other like-minded people.

Knowledgeable breeders carefully evaluate their own dogs and potential mates against the breed standard. Less knowledgeable breeders may choose breeding stock based only on a dog's show record. If a top-winning dog has

exaggerated traits and is used extensively as a sire, his incorrect traits can become popular and widespread, even though they are contrary to the breed standard and detrimental to the integrity of the breed. Judges need to reward correct traits, not what is popular.

A conformation dog show is not a comparison of one dog to another. It is a comparison of each dog to the breed standard.

Registries

AKC - American Kennel Club
The largest registry of purebred dogs in the United States.

FCI - The Fédération Cynologique Internationale
(English: International Canine Federation). The largest international federation of national kennel clubs that includes kennel clubs from across Europe as well as Africa, the Americas, Asia and Oceania.

ASCA - Australian Shepherd Club of America
Established as the parent club for Australian Shepherds in 1957. The largest independent breed-specific club in the United States.

Bred to
be Athletic

DORIEN VOGELAAR PHOTOGRAPHY

GARY DEPP PHOTOGRAPHY

BECKY PARKER / DALLY UP PHOTOGRAPHY

Functional structure for livestock herding dogs

Aussies and MAS need the structure and stamina to work as livestock herding dogs. The same structure is necessary for them to be dependable partners for difficult jobs such as search & rescue and to be able to compete successfully at high levels in canine sports. They need to be built for function.

It is imperative that breeders and judges adhere to the breed standards by selecting dogs with moderate structure and avoiding exaggerated traits that reduce a dog's ability to perform physically strenuous activities.

"When we stop looking at the dogs through the lens of its original purpose, be it herding, hunting, retrieving, etc., we will have created in time a distinctly different breed."
From The Australian Shepherd is Not a Trotting Breed by Jeanne Joy Hartnagle-Taylor.

AUSSIES

AKC: The Australian Shepherd has the stamina to work all day. He is attentive and animated, lithe and agile, solid and muscular without cloddiness.

FCI: He is attentive and animated, lithe and agile, solid and muscular without cloddiness.

ASCA: First and foremost, the Australian Shepherd is a true working stockdog, and anything that detracts from his usefulness as such is undesirable. The most important breed characteristics are overall moderation in size and bone, balance with correct proportions, and sound movement. The Australian Shepherd is attentive and animated, showing strength and stamina combined with unusual agility. This unusually versatile stockdog works with the power and quickness to control difficult cattle as well as the ability to move sheep without unnecessary roughness.

MAS

AKC and FCI: The Miniature American Shepherd is a small size herding dog. Exceptional agility combined with strength and stamina allows for working over a variety of terrain. This highly versatile, energetic dog is an excellent athlete.

Aussies and MAS are intelligent working dogs with strong herding and guarding instincts. They are good-natured, devoted, and loyal companions.

AUSSIES

AKC: The Australian Shepherd is an intelligent working dog of strong herding and guarding instincts. He is a loyal companion and has the stamina to work all day. He is an intelligent, active dog with an even disposition; he is good natured, seldom quarrelsome. He may be somewhat reserved in initial meetings. Faults - Any display of shyness, fear or aggression is to be severely penalized.

FCI: The Australian Shepherd is an intelligent working dog of strong herding and guarding instincts. He is a loyal companion and has the stamina to work all day. With an even disposition, he is good natured, seldom quarrelsome. He may be somewhat reserved in initial meetings. All Australian Shepherds show an unsurpassed devotion to their families.

ASCA: The Australian Shepherd is primarily a working dog of strong herding and guardian instincts. He is an intelligent, exceptional companion. He is versatile and easily trained: performing his assigned tasks with great style and enthusiasm. He is reserved with strangers but does not exhibit shyness. Although an aggressive, authoritative worker, viciousness toward people or animals is intolerable.

MAS

AKC and FCI: Superior intelligence and a willingness to please those to whom he is devoted. He is both a loyal companion and a biddable worker, which is evident in his watchful expression. An exceptional companion, he is versatile and easily trained, performing his assigned tasks with great style and enthusiasm. Although reserved with strangers, he does not exhibit shyness. He is a resilient and persistent worker, who adjusts his demeanor and arousal appropriately to the task at hand. With his family he is protective, good natured, devoted and loyal.

ROCK: Livestock herding

OLIVIA FROST PHOTO

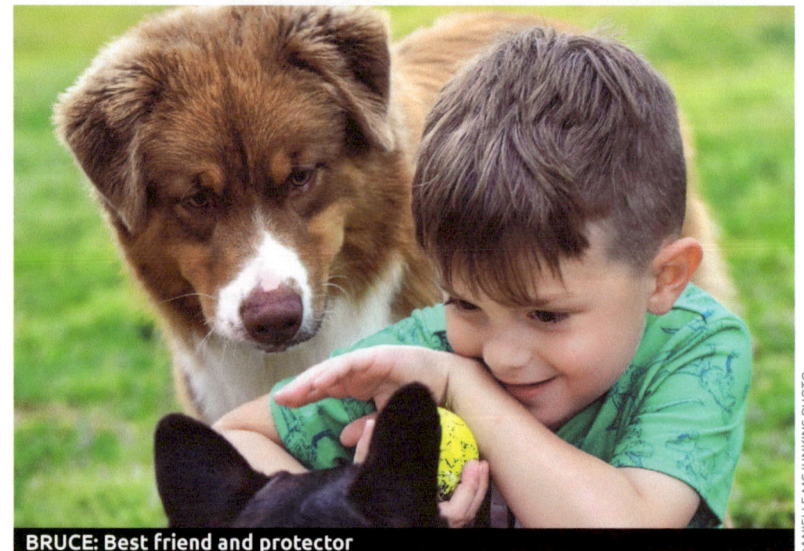

BRUCE: Best friend and protector

DANIELLE MCJUNKINS PHOTO

Strong herding and guarding instincts. Good-natured, devoted, loyal.

Moderation is the single most important quality of these breeds

It is vital to select dogs that are structurally sound and capable of demonstrating the speed, coordination, and agility necessary for the tasks which the dog will be asked to perform.

Moderation in size and substance are fundamental traits. If everything else is equal, a heavier dog is unlikely to run as fast or have the same endurance as a lighter dog of the same height. However, a dog that lacks substance may not have adequate muscular strength to accomplish difficult tasks.

Aussies and MAS were developed as stockdogs. They require moderate structure:

- for quick acceleration to turn back livestock.
- for agility to dodge horns and kicking hooves.
- to alter gait instantly to outmaneuver livestock.
- for strength and stamina to work all day on rough terrain during rain, sleet, snow, and under hot sun.

Aussies and MAS are also very popular as canine sport dogs and family companions. They require moderate structure:

- to accelerate quickly, run at top speed, and maneuver rapidly through agility and flyball courses.
- to alter gait, turn abruptly, and leap high when catching a ball or disc.
- for stamina to train hard for all sports and to keep up with active families.

DUKE: Livestock herding

SUSAN LAWLEY SEVERNS PHOTOGRAPHY

TURBO: Disc dog

ANNETTE SHAFF PHOTOGRAPHY / SHUTTERSTOCK

SMOOCH: Agility

SASCHA VADAGNIN PHOTOGRAPHY

RIBBON: Playing ball

OLIVIA FROST PHOTO

The moderate structure and athletic ability necessary for livestock herding are also necessary for other working tasks, many popular dog sports, and life as a family dog.

Aussies and MAS need to be agile, structurally sound, and totally functional

Undesirable features include:

Head

- large, domed head with exaggerated stop
- "baby-face" or "teddy bear" look and expression
- long, narrow head with snipey muzzle
- protruding, round, or sunken eyes
- excess skin around eyes and lips
- large, heavy, low-set ears with no lift

Body

- excess coat and excess bone, or too little bone
- chest too wide, too narrow, or shallow
- ribcage or loin too long
- legs too short
- sloping topline
- excess rear angulation

Movement

- exaggerated kick-up in rear movement
- excess lifting of front legs and feet when trotting
- exaggerated reach and drive

Exaggerated sidegait is an artificial gait designed to win in the show ring. It is not a functional working gait and is not appropriate for Aussies and MAS.

Preserving the integrity of the breeds means avoiding exaggerations and choosing dogs with moderate structure.

DOC: Livestock herding

SUSAN SEVERNS PHOTOGRAPHY

BLOOM: Agility

GINGER & BLACK PHOTOGRAPHY

Moderate structure is necessary for quick acceleration and the flexibility to maneuver instantly in any direction.

Aussies and MAS work hard at many jobs

Because of their physical stamina, moderate size, high intelligence, and eagerness to learn, Aussies and MAS are prized for the work they perform. One of their indispensable qualities is the drive to keep working when the going gets tough, even after being injured. Some of the jobs they perform to help their human partners include:

- herding, ranch, and farm dogs
- alert dogs for cancer, diabetes, migraines, and seizures
- assistance dogs for the disabled
- canine defense
- crisis response
- hearing assistance dogs
- police work
- scent detection for agricultural products, bombs, cash, contraband, and drugs
- search and rescue
- seeing-eye dogs
- therapy dogs
- water rescue
- and many other capacities.

LOLA: Water rescue training

JINDRICH HANACEK PHOTOGRAPHY

MAC: Canine defense

MICHELLE BESTER PHOTOGRAPHY

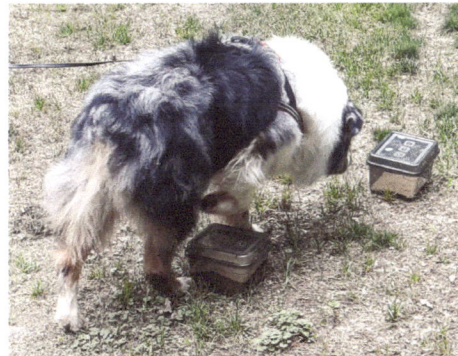

GRIFF: Scent detection

KAY MARKS PHOTO

MCGYVER: Search and rescue

RICK STEIN PHOTO

ANDREW: Livestock herding

BECKY PARKER, DALLY UP PHOTOGRAPHY

HAWK: Crisis response, 911 World Trade Towers

MISSOURI TASK FORCE 1 PHOTO

Aussies and MAS excel in canine sports

Athletic structure along with superior intelligence and trainability make them truly versatile for:

- agility
- canicross trail running
- disc
- dock diving
- flyball
- freestyle dancing
- lure coursing
- obedience
- rally
- sled racing and ski-jouring
- tracking
- trick dogs
- and all-around companions.

They enjoy these activities and are willing to do almost everything asked of them.

APPLEDORE TEAM: Dog sled

DIANA MINGALIEVA PHOTO

TESS: Disc dog

LINDSEY THOMPSON PHOTOGRAPHY

ZIGGY: Flyball

JIM GEISER PHOTO

NEYLA: Agility

CLAUDIA BOSSELMANN PHOTO

BLIZZ: Agility

DORIEN VOGELAAR PHOTOGRAPHY

Like **THIS**

Like **THIS**

AMBER JADE AANENSEN PHOTOGRAPHY

ANNE FRANÇOISE PHOTOGRAPHY

AUSSIES

AKC and FCI: Solidly built with moderate bone. Structure in the male reflects masculinity without coarseness. Bitches appear feminine without being slight of bone.

ASCA: Masculinity or femininity is well defined.

MAS

AKC: Solidly built with moderate bone in proportion to body height and size. Structure in the dog reflects masculinity without coarseness. Bitches appear feminine without being slight of bone.

FCI: Same wording as AKC with this addition: The overall structure gives an impression of depth and strength without bulkiness.

Not **THAT**

Not **THAT**

SHUTTERSTOCK

SHUTTERSTOCK

Not THAT — SQUARE

Like THIS — CORRECT

Not THAT — TOO LONG

BODY LENGTH: AUSSIES

AKC and FCI: Measuring from the breastbone to rear of thigh and from top of the withers to the ground, the Australian Shepherd is slightly longer than tall. **ASCA:** Well-balanced, slightly longer than tall.

BODY LENGTH: MAS

AKC and FCI: Measuring from the point of the shoulder to the point of the buttocks and from the highest point of the shoulder blade to the ground, he is slightly longer than tall.

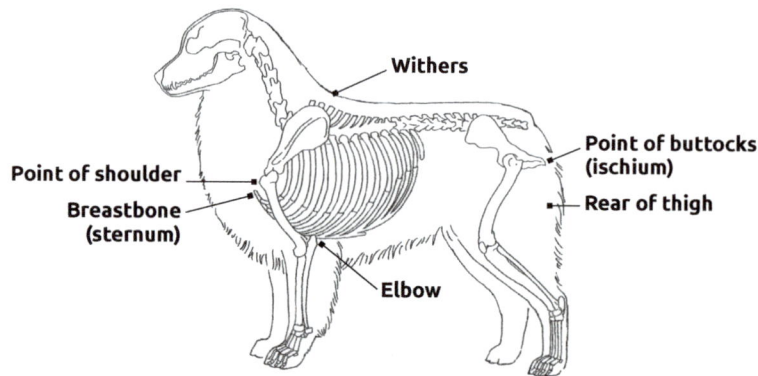

Withers

Point of shoulder

Breastbone (sternum)

Elbow

Point of buttocks (ischium)

Rear of thigh

Like THIS — Correct leg length

Not THAT — Legs too short (manipulated photo)

JULIA BETTENDORF PHOTOGRAPHY

VERA REVA PHOTOGRAPHY / SHUTTERSTOCK

LEG LENGTH: AUSSIES

AKC and FCI: Not mentioned. **ASCA:** The point of the elbow is set under the withers and is equidistant from the withers to the ground.

LEG LENGTH: MAS

AKC and FCI: The elbow joint is equidistant from the ground to the withers.

Like
THIS

AUSTRALIAN SHEPHERDS
All standards
Preferred heights

NO SIZE DISQUALIFICATION

MALES
Maximum 23 inches (58 cm)
Minimum 20 inches (51 cm)

FEMALES
Maximum 21 inches (53 cm)
Minimum 18 inches (46 cm)

Quality is not to be sacrificed in favor of size.

MINIATURE AMERICAN SHEPHERDS
All standards
Designated heights

DISQUALIFICATION: OVER OR UNDER SIZE

MALES
Maximum 18 inches (46 cm)
Minimum 14 inches (35.5 cm)

FEMALES
Maximum 17 inches (43.5 cm)
Minimum 13 inches (33 cm)

A healthy weight will be based on individual height, gender, and substance.

AUSSIE: Large male 23" (58 cm)
(green lines max. and min. heights)

AUSSIE: Small female 18" (46 cm)
(yellow lines max. and min. heights)

MAS: Large male 18" (46cm)
(green lines max. and min. heights)

MAS: Small female 13" (33 cm)
(yellow lines max. and min. heights)

AMBER JADE ANNENSEN PHOTOGRAPHY

Head
Strong and Expressive

DEFINITION OF CLEAN CUT: Chiseled outline

DEFINITION OF DRY: Neat and tidy with no loose skin

AUSSIES

AKC: The head is clean cut, strong and dry. Overall size should be in proportion to the body. The muzzle is equal in length or slightly shorter than the back skull. Viewed from the side the topline of the back skull and muzzle form parallel planes, divided by a moderate, well-defined stop. Skull: Top flat to slightly domed. It may show a slight occipital protuberance.* Length and width are equal. Moderate well-defined stop.

FCI: The head is clean cut, strong and dry. Overall size should be in proportion to the body. Skull: Top flat to slightly domed. It may show a slight occipital protuberance.* Length and width are equal. Stop: Moderate, well-defined.

ASCA: The head is clean-cut, strong, dry, and in proportion to the body. The topskull is flat to slightly rounded; its length and width each equal to the length of the muzzle. The toplines of the muzzle and topskull appear close to parallel. The stop is moderate but well defined.

MAS

AKC and FCI: The head is clean-cut, dry, and in proportion to the body. Skull: The crown is flat to slightly round and may show a slight occipital protuberance.* The width and the length of the crown are equal. Stop: The stop is moderate but defined. Planes: Viewed from the side, the muzzle and the top line of the crown are slightly oblique to each other, with the front of the crown on a slight angle downward toward the nose.

***The occipital protuberance (or occiput)** is a knob-like bump at the back of the skull. It is part of the occipital bone which protects the brain and supports the muscles and ligaments of the neck.

Like THIS

JJ RANCH PHOTO

Like THIS

LAS ROCOSA PHOTO

DAVE BIRREN PHOTO

JULIA BETTENDORF PHOTOGRAPHY

AUSSIES

AKC: Viewed from the side the topline of the back skull and muzzle form parallel planes, divided by a moderate, well-defined stop. Skull: Top flat to slightly domed. It may show a slight occipital protuberance.* (Smooth down hair to check plane of topskull.)

FCI: Viewed from the side the topline of the back skull and muzzle form parallel planes, divided by a moderate, well-defined stop. Skull: Top flat to slightly domed. It may show a slight occipital protuberance.*

ASCA: The topskull is flat to slightly rounded. The toplines of the muzzle and topskull appear close to parallel. The stop is moderate but well defined.

MAS

AKC and FCI: Skull: The crown is flat to slightly round and may show a slight occipital protuberance.*
Stop: The stop is moderate but defined. Planes: Viewed from the side, the muzzle and the top line of the crown are slightly oblique to each other, with the front of the crown on a slight angle downward toward the nose.

*The occipital protuberance (or occiput) is a knob-like bump at the back of the skull. It is part of the occipital bone which protects the brain and supports the muscles and ligaments of the neck.

Like THIS

PHOTO COURTESY OF DIANA HEFTI

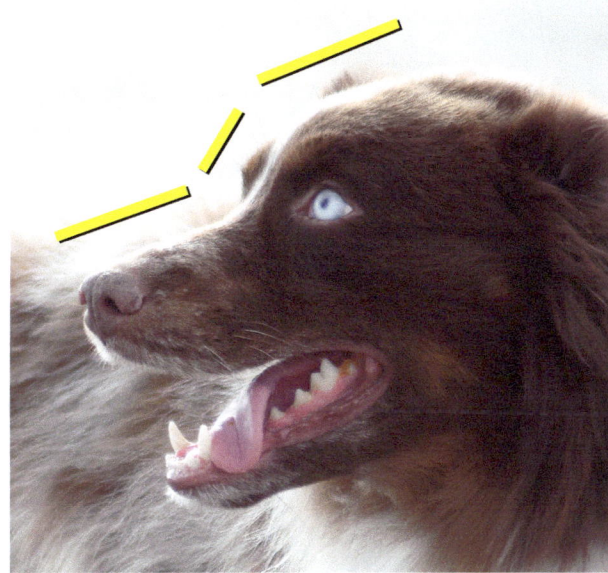

PHOTO COURTESY OF CHRISTINA MISTRETTA

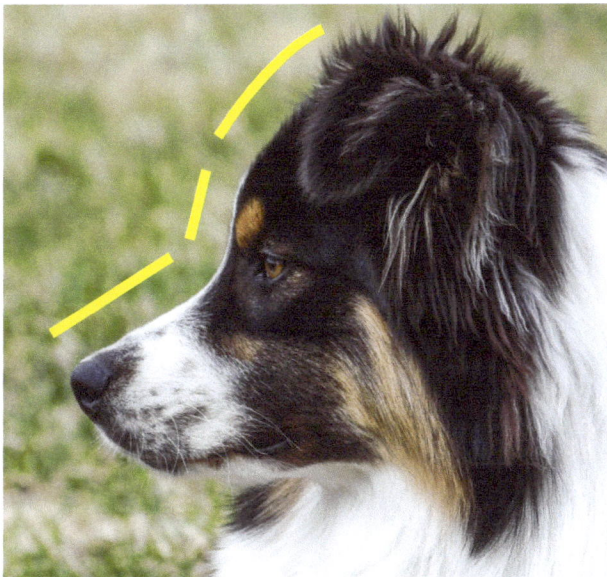

PAULA MCDERMID PHOTO

The dog immediately above has thick fur on top of his head which should be smoothed down to check his true skull shape.

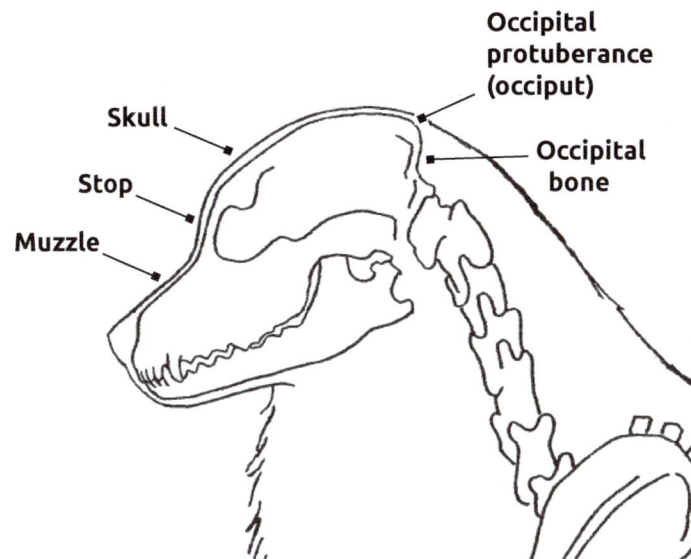

Skull

Stop

Muzzle

Occipital protuberance (occiput)

Occipital bone

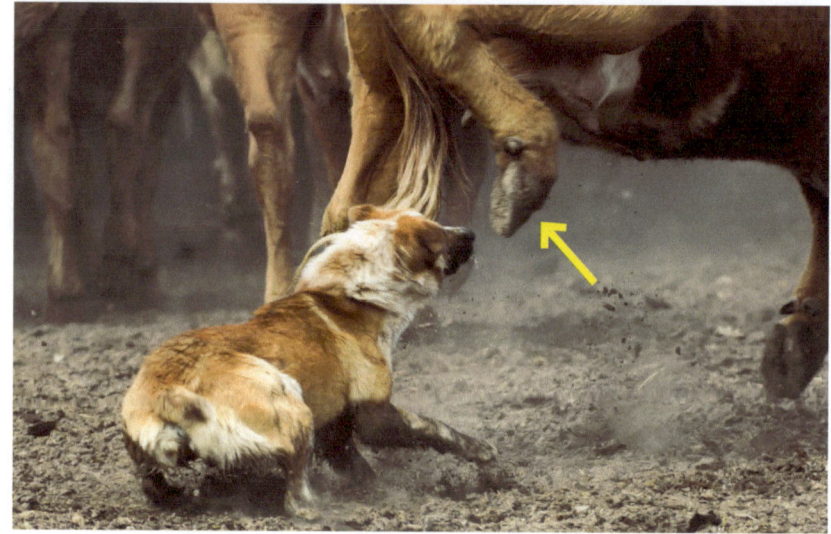

Like
THIS

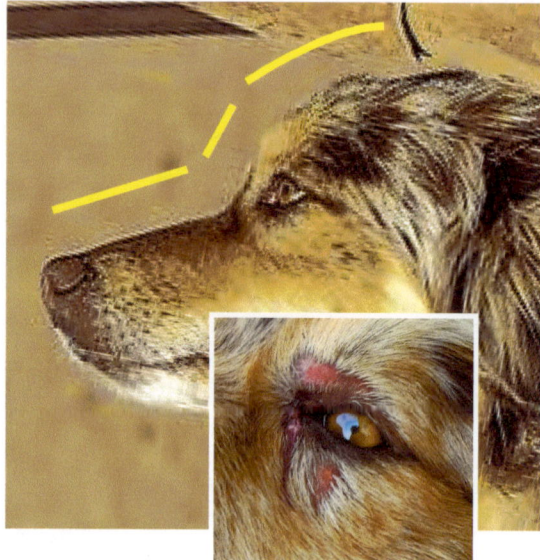

SUSAN BOYD PHOTOGRAPHY

The primary purpose of the skull is to protect the brain and vital senses of sight, scent and hearing

This Australian Shepherd was rounding up range cattle with his owner, who was on horseback. When their job was finished and his owner was unsaddling her horse, she noticed that the skin above and below the dog's eye was scraped. He had been kicked by a cow.

The abrasion on his skin was superficial and healed rapidly. The eye was not damaged because his speed and agility enabled him to drop to the ground swiftly, and his correct head structure allowed the cow's hoof to glance off.

Head structure determines eye placement and field of vision

Correct head construction places the eyes at the ideal depth and angle so that each breed has the best field of vision for its purpose. Aussies and MAS have the right combination of peripheral vision and central vision for livestock herding tasks.

Stockdogs must be able to detect the slightest movements of livestock out of the corners of their eyes. They have only split-seconds to react in situations that could cause them serious injury or death. Correct head construction provides a wide field of vision that enables a dog to see and react instantly, and it creates a protective structure for the vital senses.

For dogs who have working jobs, compete in canine sports, or are family dogs, correct head structure can help minimize injury to the brain, eyes, and other vital senses from a blow to the head or collision with an object.

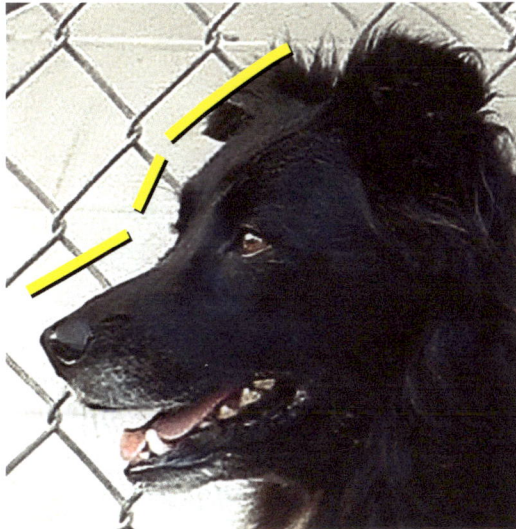

TERRY MARTIN PHOTOGRAPHY

Not **THAT**

PIXABAY

Correct head planes as described in the breed standards

This dog's backskull is flat and the stop is moderate but well-defined. Note: Eyebrows protrude above the stop, so be sure to look at the angle that is *between* the eyebrows.

This solidly-constructed head has the correct shape and profile as described in the breed standards. This head was developed over many decades by ranchers who knew exactly which structure was the most functional and durable for a stockdog.

In contrast, notice the domed skull, exaggerated steep stop, and short muzzle of the blue merle at right.

Wide, domed skull and steep stop

When breeders select for wide skulls instead of moderate skulls, the cheek bones become wider and the eye sockets and eyes rotate slighty forward. The eyes are less protected in this position. A domed backskull and steep stop make the head more vulnerable to injury.

- The exaggerated shape may catch a flying hoof or other object, putting the dog at risk for severe damage to the brain and vital senses.

- A domed "blocky" head is undesirable, but it is a current trend. The expression is cute like a Teddy Bear, which is not correct. The expression of Aussies and Miniature Americans should be keen and intelligent.

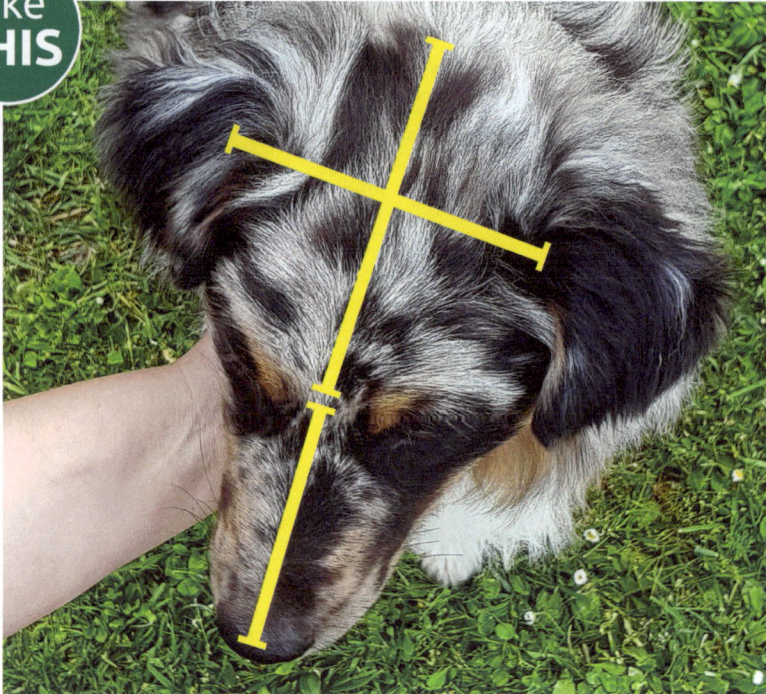

Like THIS

PAULA MCDERMID PHOTO

Like THIS

AMBER JADE AANENSEN PHOTOGRAPHY

Head Proportions

AUSSIES

AKC: Skull length and width are equal. Muzzle is equal in length or slightly shorter than the back skull.

FCI: Length and width (of skull) are equal. Muzzle: Equal in length or slightly shorter than the back skull.

ASCA: The head length and width each equal to the length of the muzzle.

MAS

AKC and FCI: The width and the length of the crown are equal.

WHY? These proportions define the ideal head shape so that they don't become too short and wide or too long and narrow.

Muzzle Shape

AUSSIES

AKC and FCI: The muzzle tapers little from base to nose and is rounded at the tip.

ASCA: Medium width and depth and tapers gradually to a rounded tip, without appearing heavy or snipey.

MAS

AKC and FCI: The muzzle is of medium width and depth and tapers gradually to a rounded tip without appearing heavy, square, snipy, or loose. Length is equal to the length of the crown.

Like
THIS

CHERYL NAKAKURA PHOTO

Like
THIS

JC DOG PHOTOGRAPHY.NET

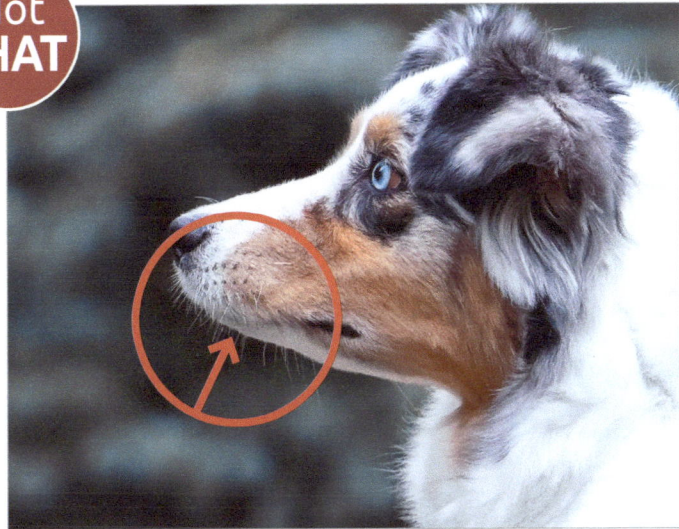

Not
THAT

DENIS NATA PHOTO / SHUTTERSTOCK

Definition of Strong Head

- Solid bone structure of skull.

- Strong, protective bone around the eyes.

- Correct muzzle length, width, and fullness.

- Deep underjaw that provides strong bone to firmly anchor teeth. The well-developed underjaw, rounded at the chin, should extend close to the base of the nostril.

- Stockdogs need a strong head and underjaw for gripping stock and to minimize injury to the head, muzzle, and teeth from the impact of a kick.

- Dogs who are work partners, competitors in canine sports, and family dogs require a strong head to minimize injury from a blow to the head or collision with an object.

AUSSIES

AKC and FCI: Eyes almond shaped, not protruding nor sunken.

ASCA: Eyes are clear, almond-shaped, of moderate size, and set a little obliquely, neither prominent nor sunken.

MAS

AKC AND FCI: Eyes are set obliquely, almond shaped, neither protruding nor sunken and in proportion to the head.

Snug skin around the eyes

- The skin around the eyes should be snug for best protection of the eyeballs. The eyeball itself is round, the snug skin creates the characteristic almond shape and correct expression.

- Normal eyelids provide lubrication, keep the eyes clean, and help protect them from being injured by wind, debris, or trauma.

- Dogs have three eyelids in each eye. Between the upper and lower eyelids, a third eyelid is hidden in the inner corner of the eye. The third eyelid is a triangular membrane of conjunctival tissue that sweeps across the surface of the eye to remove debris, provide protection, and to distribute tear film. The third eyelid is not always visible or only a small portion may be visible.

WHY is loose skin around the eyes undesirable?

- When the skin of the head is loose or the lower eyelid muscles are weak, the lower eyelid can droop down and roll away from the eye, exposing the delicate inner eyelid tissue. This is called a **haw or ectropion**.

- Eyes can be damaged if seeds, dirt, or debris are trapped in the haws.

- Conspicuous haws expose the delicate tissues of the inner surface of the eyelids, causing the tissues to become dry. The surface of the eye or the cornea may also dry out, causing inflammation, scarring, and impaired vision. These conditions are painful to the dog and reduce his quality of life.

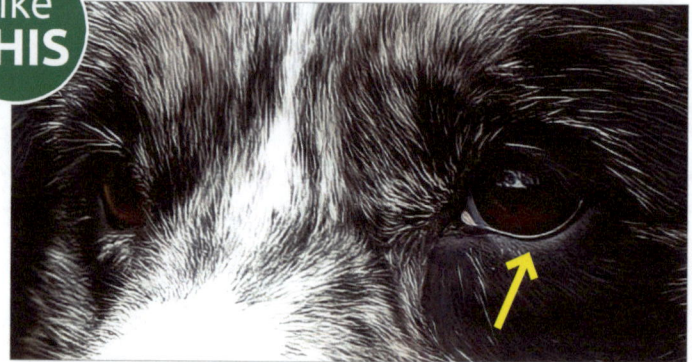

Snug skin around the eyes creates the desired almond shape.

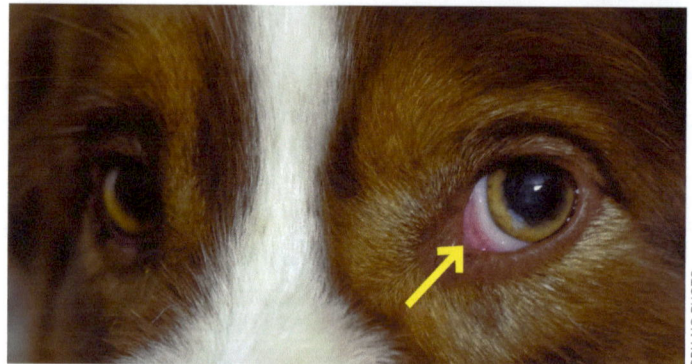

Normal eye showing the pink third eyelid.

Prominent haws (ectropion) can cause eye tissue to become dry and may lead to serious eye problems.

Definition Of Dry Mouth

No extra or loose skin around the mouth

- **DRY** refers to tight lips.
- Loose, sagging lips are called flews, wet lips, or wet mouth.
- Tight lips create a straight, clean lipline.
- Upper and lower lips should meet and fit smoothly together all the way around the muzzle.

AUSSIES

AKC: Not mentioned.

FCI: Not mentioned.

ASCA: Lips are close fitting, meeting at the mouthline.

MAS

AKC: Not mentioned.

FCI: Lips to be tight fitting.

WHY is loose skin around the mouth undesirable?

- Loose, sagging lips (flews) can become snagged and torn during conflict with other animals.
- Detracts from correct breed type.

Like **THIS**

PIXABAY

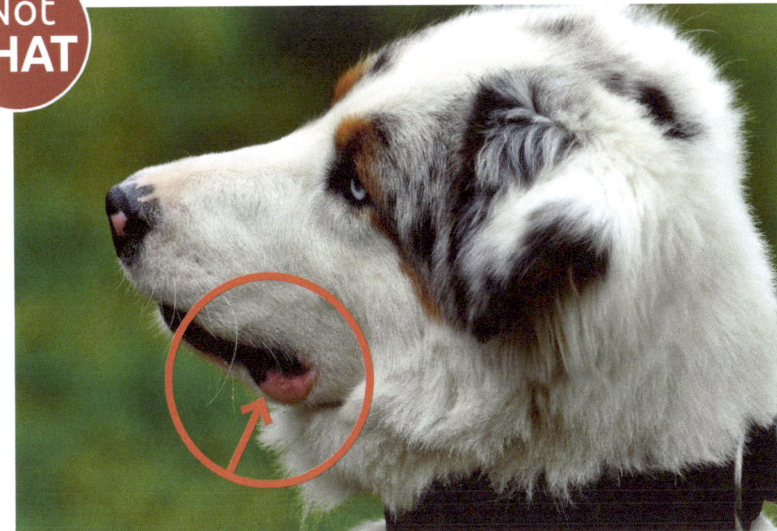

Not **THAT**

PIXABAY

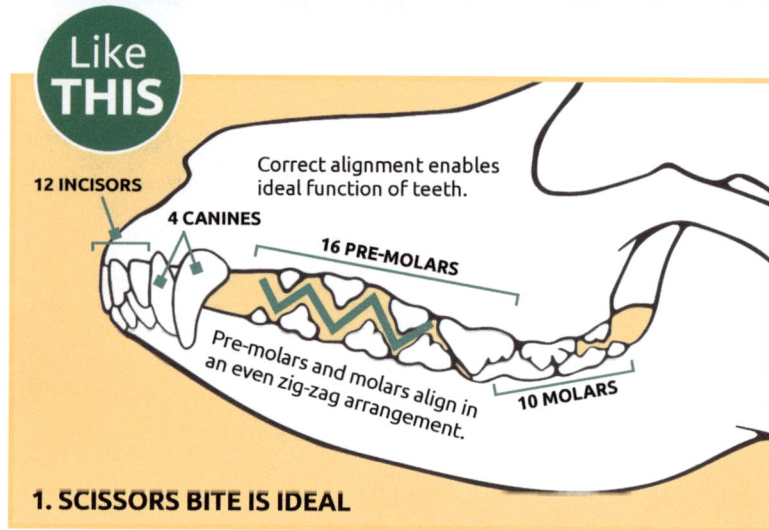

Like THIS

12 INCISORS

4 CANINES

16 PRE-MOLARS

Correct alignment enables ideal function of teeth.

Pre-molars and molars align in an even zig-zag arrangement.

10 MOLARS

PAULA MCDERMID

1. SCISSORS BITE IS IDEAL

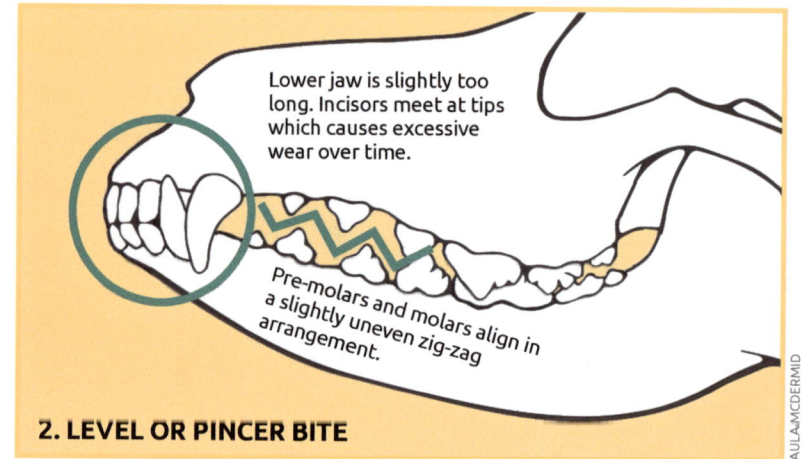

Lower jaw is slightly too long. Incisors meet at tips which causes excessive wear over time.

Pre-molars and molars align in a slightly uneven zig-zag arrangement.

PAULA MCDERMID

2. LEVEL OR PINCER BITE

AUSSIES

AKC and FCI: A full complement of strong white teeth should meet in a scissors bite or may meet in a level bite. (FCI: pincer bite.)

DISQUALIFICATIONS: Undershot. Overshot greater than 1/8 inch. Loss of contact caused by short center incisors in an otherwise correct bite shall not be judged undershot. Teeth broken or missing by accident shall not be penalized.

ASCA: A full complement of strong white teeth meet in a scissors bite. A level bite is a fault. Teeth broken or missing by accident are not penalized. All other missing teeth should be faulted to the degree that they deviate from a full complement of 42 teeth.

DISQUALIFICATIONS: Undershot bite, overshot bite, wry mouth.

MAS

AKC and FCI: A full complement of teeth meet in a scissor bite. Teeth broken, missing or discoloured by accident are not penalized.

DISQUALIFICATIONS: Undershot or overshot bite.

Faulty jaw development is usually hereditary and affected dogs should not be used for breeding. It is unethical to show a dog in conformation if orthodontics were performed to correct a genetically disqualifying bite.

SCISSORS BITE : Ideal (illustration 1)

- The lower **incisors** (front teeth) fit tightly against the inside of the upper **incisors**. They are used for nipping, scraping meat off bones, carrying objects, and grooming the coat.
- The upper and lower **canine teeth** fit snugly together like a scissors. They are used for inflicting stabbing wounds, catching, holding, and shredding.
- **Pre-molars** are used for tearing and chewing. When using these teeth, dogs often tilt their head to one side.
- **Molars** are used for shearing, crushing, and grinding. When the jaws are properly aligned, the pre-molars and molars are arranged in an even zig-zag pattern.

LEVEL OR PINCER BITE (illustration 2)

AUSSIES: Acceptable. MAS: Deviation from ideal.

- The upper and lower **incisors** (front teeth) meet at their tips. This bite is functional but causes excess wear on the incisors over time. The incisors may have worn down to stumps in old dogs.
- Alignment of teeth behind the canines (**pre-molars** and **molars**) is functional but not ideal. The teeth are able to crush and chew; the slight misalignment causes their surfaces to wear unevenly.

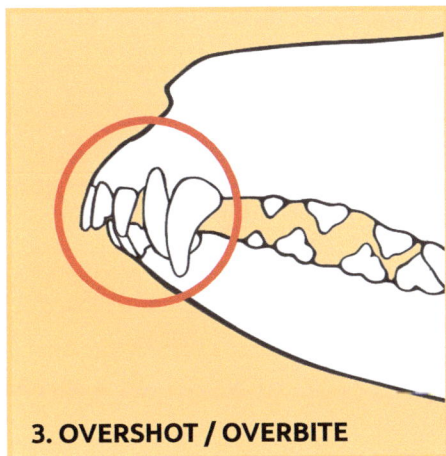

OVERSHOT / OVERBITE

- Upper jaw is longer than lower jaw. Upper incisors protrude beyond lower incisors.

- Excess overlap of canine teeth.

- Pre-molars and molars interfere with each other.

3. OVERSHOT / OVERBITE

PAULA McDERMID

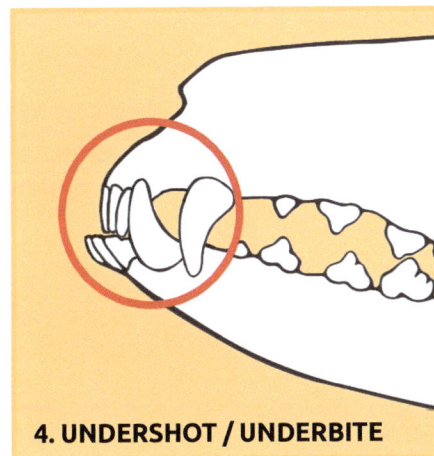

UNDERSHOT / UNDERBITE

- Lower jaw is longer than upper jaw. Lower incisors protrude beyond upper incisors.

- Gap between canine teeth

- Pre-molars and molars interfere with each other.

4. UNDERSHOT / UNDERBITE

PAULA McDERMID

Bite problems are not just about the front teeth

With a few exceptions, such as trauma, the relationship of the upper and lower jaws determines the bite and affects the alignment of **all** the teeth. Dogs have two parts to the upper jaw (left and right sides) and two parts to the lower jaw (left and right sides). All four jaw parts grow independently which can cause alignment problems.

Most commonly, **overshot** and **undershot** bites are caused by top and bottom jaws of mismatched lengths. A **wry mouth** occurs when one side of the jaw is longer than the other side, resulting in a crooked, angled bite. **Asymmetry from side-to-side** occurs when jaws are not centered over each other at the midline.

OVERSHOT BITE: Disqualification (illustration 3)

- The lower jaw is shorter than the upper jaw. The upper front teeth protrude beyond the lower front teeth.

- The canine teeth are misaligned, and depending on the severity of the misalignment, can cause the lower canine teeth and lower incisors to press into the roof of the mouth and gum tissue of the upper jaw, causing pain and damaging teeth.

- The pre-molars and molars interfere with each other, which can cause difficulty chewing and abnormal wear of the teeth.

UNDERSHOT BITE: Disqualification (illustration 4)

- The upper jaw is shorter than the lower jaw. The lower front teeth protrude beyond the upper front teeth. This can cause the upper incisors to press into the gum tissue of the lower jaws.

- The canine teeth are also misaligned, which can cause damage if they scrape against the incisors or press into the gum tissue.

- The pre-molars and molars interfere with each other, which can cause difficulty chewing and abnormal wear of the teeth.

Why Does It Matter?

- Disqualifying bites are not functional. In addition to possible pain and damage to teeth and gums, a dog with a significant overshot or undershot bite may not be able to eat properly, may not be able to pull burrs out of his own feet, a bitch is less able to chew umbilical cords during whelping, and a stockdog can't grip livestock properly.

- A correct jaw with a scissors bite closes tightly like a zipper along the entire length of the jaw. This structure can minimize damage to the teeth and muzzle if the dog receives a blow to the head, such as from a kick by a cow or collision with an object.

- A truly functional bite wears evenly and requires minimal dental intervention over the lifetime of the dog.

Like **THIS**

PAULA WATERMAN/INKWELL STUDIO PHOTO

Like **THIS**

ANNE FRANÇOISE PHOTOGRAPHY

AUSSIES

AKC and FCI: The blue merles and blacks have black pigmentation on eye rims. The red merles and reds have liver (brown) pigmentation on eye rims. Nose - Blue merles and blacks have black pigmentation on the nose (and lips). Red merles and reds have liver (brown) pigmentation on the nose (and lips).

ASCA: The blue merle and black have black pigmentation on nose, lips and eye-rims. Reds and red merles have liver pigmentation on nose, lips and eye rims.

MAS

AKC and FCI: The eye rims of the reds and red merles have full red (liver) pigmentation. The eye rims of the blacks and blue merles have full black pigmentation. Nose - Red merles and reds have red (liver) pigmentation on the nose leather. Blue merles and blacks have black pigmentation on the nose leather. Fully pigmented noses are preferred.

FCI adds: Lips: Pigment to match colour of dog.

Liver pigmentation on the nose, lips, and eye rims of reds and red merles is required. A dog who appears to be red but has black pigment on nose, eye rims, and lips could be genetically yellow or this could indicate mongrelization.

AUSSIES

AKC and FCI: On the merles it is permissible to have small pink spots; however, they should not exceed 25% of the nose on dogs over one year of age, which is a **SERIOUS FAULT.**

ASCA: Butterfly nose should not be faulted under one year of age. (A butterfly nose is a pink nose with various amounts of dark pigment. Often the nose will fill in with pigment as the dog matures.)

ASCA: Dudley nose is a **DISQUALIFICATION.** (A Dudley nose is pink with no dark pigment.)

MAS

AKC and FCI: Fully pigmented noses are preferred.

NOSES that are less than fully pigmented will be **FAULTED.**

SEVERE FAULT: 25% to 50% un-pigmented nose leather.

DISQUALIFICATION: Over 50% un-pigmented nose leather.

DEFINITIONS

Butterfly nose
A pink nose with various amounts of dark pigment.
Dudley nose
A pink nose with no dark pigment.

WHY is pink nose leather undesirable?

Pink noses are at higher risk of sun damage, which can potentially become cancerous. This is highly undesirable for dogs who spend a significant amount of time outdoors.

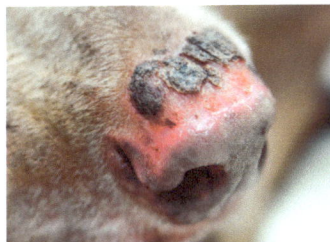

Sun damage

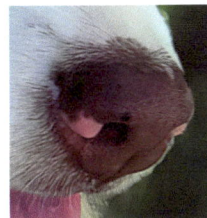

LESS THAN 25% UNPIGMENTED NOSE

AUSSIES: AKC, FCI, ASCA: Permissible on merles under 1 year of age.
MAS: AKC, FCI: FAULT. Fully pigmented noses are preferred.

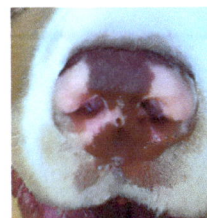

25% TO 50% UNPIGMENTED NOSE

AUSSIES: AKC, FCI: SERIOUS FAULT on dogs over 1 year of age.
ASCA: FAULT.
MAS: AKC, FCI: SEVERE FAULT.

MORE THAN 50% UNPIGMENTED NOSE

AUSSIES: AKC, FCI: All three photos are a **SERIOUS FAULT** on dogs over 1 year of age.
ASCA: Left two photos: **FAULT.** Far right photo: **DISQUALIFICATION.**
MAS: AKC, FCI: All three photos are a **DISQUALIFICATION.**

PAULA MCDERMID PHOTO

Eyes
Expression
Ears

Like
THIS

One or both eyes may be brown, blue, hazel, amber, or any colour combination, including flecks and marbling.

Acceptable in ALL coat colours.

AUSSIES

AKC and FCI: Eyes are brown, blue, amber or any variation or combination thereof, including flecks and marbling. Almond shaped, not protruding nor sunken.

ASCA: Clear, almond-shaped, of moderate size, and set a little obliquely, neither prominent nor sunken. The pupils are dark, well defined, and perfectly positioned. Eye colour is brown, blue, amber, or any variation or combination, including flecks and marbling. All eye colours are acceptable in combination with all coat colours. **FAULT:** Any deviation from almond-shaped eyes.

MAS

AKC and FCI: Eyes are set obliquely, almond-shaped, neither protruding nor sunken and in proportion to the head. Acceptable in all coat colours, one or both eyes may be brown, blue, hazel, amber or any colour combination thereof, including flecks and marbling.

DEFINITION

Oblique eye
The outer corner of the eye is higher than the inner corner.

JEKATERINA PARIJENKO PHOTOGRAPHY

PAULA MCDERMID PHOTO

MICHAEL TWESTEN PHOTOGRAPHY

PENNY BROOKS, PENZ PHOTOZ

Blue eyes are correct and equally desirable in all coat colours, including blue merle, black, red merle, and red.

HELENE NILSEN PHOTO

MARY ARNOLD PHOTO

Marbled eyes

In merles, eyes can be marbled with flecks and blotches of brown, amber, or blue. Marbling occurs in the iris (the coloured area in the eye). The pupil (the black center of the eye) is perfectly round in shape. Marbling should not be confused with iris coloboma.

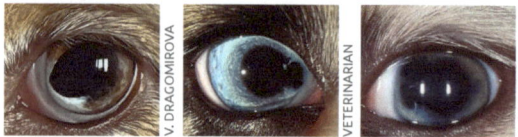

V. DRAGOMIROVA

VETERINARIAN

C. PELTIER

Iris coloboma and iris hypoplasia

Marbled eyes and iris colobomas can appear somewhat similar. However, an **iris coloboma** is a defect that may look like an irregularly-shaped pupil or a notch or hole in the iris.

A related defect is **iris hypoplasia**, which is a thinning of the iris tissue. Iris coloboma and iris hypoplasia occur when part of the iris fails to develop before birth. These eye defects can be inherited.

ANNE FRANÇOISE PHOTO

TATRANSKÁ LABKA

MARCO ROSETTI PHOTOGRAPHY

HAYLEY LAMB PHOTO

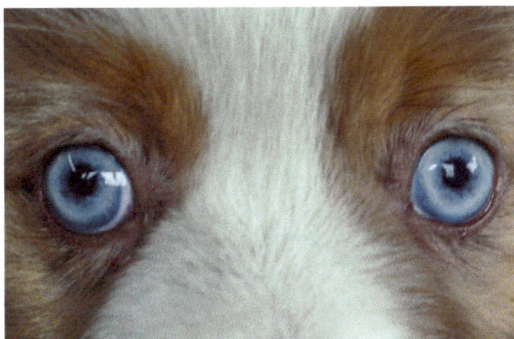

Round eyes

Protruding eyes

Drooping lower eyelids (haws or ectropion)

Eyes should be almond-shaped

Eye shape faults are caused by incorrect head structure resulting in poorly-positioned eyes and eye sockets.

Drooping lower eyelids (haws or ectropion) can be caused by loose skin on the head or weak lower eyelid muscles.

Faults

- **All standards:** Round, protruding, or sunken eyes.
- **All standards except FCI MAS:** Loose skin around the eyes that causes the lower eyelids to sag. Standards say "Head clean cut, strong and dry" which means no excess skin.

WHY?

- Protruding eyes are vulnerable to injury from debris and physical trauma.
- Drooping lower eyelids (haws/ectropion) expose the delicate tissue of the inner eyelid, which can result in painful corneal inflammation, corneal scarring, and impaired vision. Haws can trap seeds, dirt, and debris that can injure the eyes.
- Eyes with drooping lower eyelids (haws/ectropion), and round or bulging eyes detract from correct expression.

Correct eyes should be almond-shaped, neither protruding nor sunken.

AUSSIES

AKC and FCI: Almond-shaped, not protruding nor sunken.

ASCA: Clear, almond-shaped, of moderate size, and set a little obliquely, neither prominent nor sunken.

MAS

AKC and FCI: Eyes are set obliquely, almond-shaped, neither protruding nor sunken and in proportion to the head.

Like
THIS

What is moderate ear size?

When pulled forward gently, the tip of the ear reaches to, but not further than, the inside corner of the nearest eye.

AUSSIES

AKC: Ears are triangular, of moderate size and leather, set high on the head. At full attention they break forward and over, or to the side as a rose ear. Prick ears and hanging ears are **SEVERE FAULTS.**

FCI: Triangular, of moderate size and leather, set high on the head. At full attention they break forward and over, or to the side as a rose ear.

ASCA: The ears are set high on the side of the head, are triangular, of moderate size and slightly rounded at the tip. The tip of the ear reaches to, but not further than, the inside corner of the nearest eye. At full attention, the ears should lift from one-quarter (1/4) to one-half (1/2) above the base and break forward or slightly to the side.
SEVERE FAULTS: Prick ears; overly large ears; low set ears with no lift from the base.

MAS

AKC and FCI: Triangular, of moderate size, set high on the head. At full attention they break forward and over, or to the side as a rose ear.
SEVERE FAULTS: Prick ears and ears that hang with no lift.

CLAUDIA BOSSELMANN PHOTO

SHIELA POLK TRI-IVORY

PAULA MCDERMID PHOTO

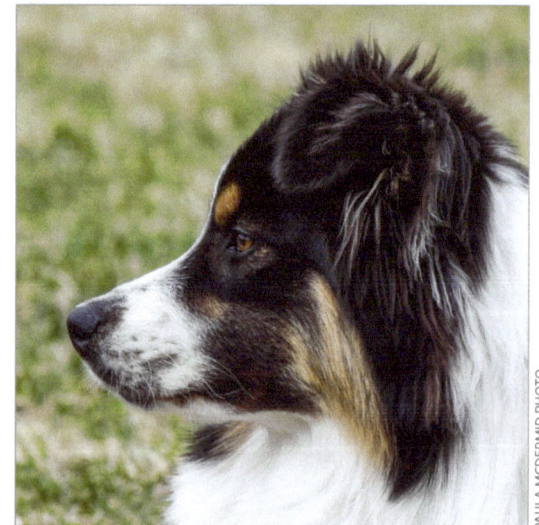

PAULA MCDERMID PHOTO

Like THIS

MARCO ROSETTI PHOTOGRAPHY

MELISSA ZOBELL BREEDER / PHOTOGRAPHER

PHOTO COURTESY OF INGA CERBULE

MARTIN SVEC PHOTOGRAPHY

PAULA MCDERMID PHOTO

PHOTO COURTESY OF MICHA BUDINSKA

AUSSIES

AKC and FCI: Showing attentiveness and intelligence, alert and eager. Gaze should be keen but friendly.

ASCA: The eyes are very expressive, showing attentiveness and intelligence.

MAS

AKC: Alert, attentive and intelligent. May express a reserved look and/or be watchful of strangers.

FCI: The expression is alert, attentive, and intelligent. They may express a reserved look or be watchful of strangers.

SHUTTERSTOCK

ISABELLE GUILLOT PHOTOGRAPHY

STARSTUFF WORKING AUSSIES PHOTO

CARITA SERVIN-HONKASALO PHOTOGRAPHY

TATRANSKÁ LABKA

Like
THIS

MARCO ROSETTI PHOTOGRAPHY

HOLLY REGINA PRESS PHOTOGRAPHY

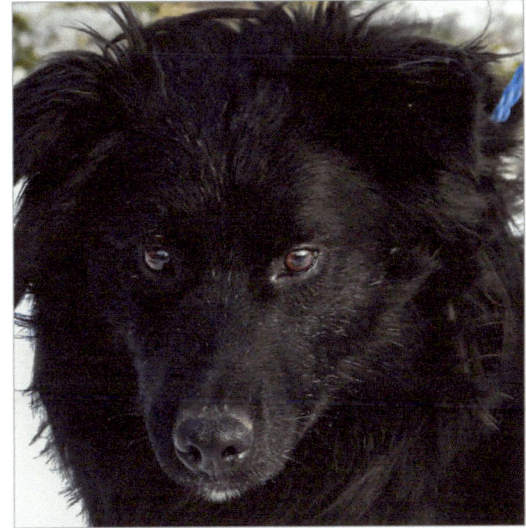

PHOTO COURTESY OF INGA CERBULE

SOUTH RAM OUFITTERS PHOTO

SOPHIE TROTIER PHOTO

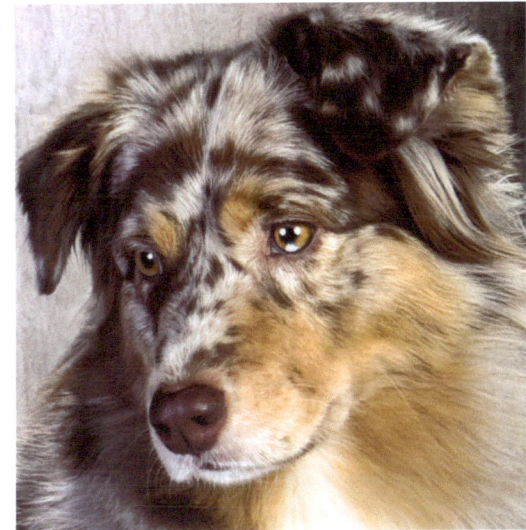

DART DOGS PHOTO / COURTESY OF RAY SCHAFER

Ears are too large. Yellow dotted lines show size the ears should be.

Low-set, hanging, hound ears

Prick ears

AUSSIES

AKC and FCI: SEVERE FAULTS: prick ears and hanging ears.

ASCA: SEVERE FAULTS: prick ears, overly large ears, low set ears with no lift from the base.

MAS

AKC and FCI: SEVERE FAULTS: prick ears and ears that hang with

no lift. **NOTE:** Prick and hound-type ears are severely faulted for detracting significantly from breed character, but are not disqualified because of the relative unimportance of earset compared to structural soundness.

Severe fault: hanging ears

WHY?

- Excess ear leather has greater risk of being torn.
- Ears with no lift are more susceptible to infection.
- Large, pendulous ears give an uncharacteristic droopy expression.

Severe fault: prick ears

WHY?

- Prick ears detract from characteristic expression.

Body
Moderate and Athletic

KERRY SPARKS / DALLY UP PHOTOGRAPHY

Like
THIS

AMBER JADE AAMJENSEN PHOTOGRAPHY

GROUP 1ST

COLUMBIANA
COUNTY
KENNEL CLUB, INC.
Jan. 7, 2022
NORTHERN OHIO WINTER CLASSIC
© jcdogphoto.net

JC DOG PHOTOGRAPHY.NET

ERIN FLEMING PHOTOGRAPHY

COURTESY SUE RITTER/BULLDOGGER PHOTO

AUSSIES

AKC and FCI: Solidly built with moderate bone. Structure in the male reflects masculinity without coarseness.
ASCA: Masculinity is well defined.

MAS

AKC: Solidly built with moderate bone in proportion to body height and size. Structure in the dog reflects masculinity without coarseness. **FCI adds:** The overall structure gives an impression of depth and strength without bulkiness.

Like
THIS

MARIA ULZUTUEVA PHOTOGRAPHY

ANNE FRANÇOISE PHOTOGRAPHY

AMBER JADE AANENSEN PHOTOGRAPHY

ANTISTUDIO PHOTOGRPHY

AUSSIES

AKC and FCI: Solidly built with moderate bone. Bitches appear feminine without being slight of bone.
ASCA: Femininity is well defined.

MAS

AKC: Solidly built with moderate bone in proportion to body height and size. Bitches appear feminine without being slight of bone. **FCI adds:** The overall structure gives an impression of depth and strength without bulkiness.

AUSSIES

AKC and FCI

Neck: Strong, of moderate length, slightly arched at the crest, fitting well into the shoulders.

Topline: Back is straight and strong, level and firm from withers to hip joints.

Croup: Moderately sloped.

Chest: Not broad but deep with the lowest point reaching the elbow.

Ribs: Well sprung and long, neither barrel chested nor slab-sided.

Underline: Shows a moderate tuck-up.

ASCA

Neck: Firm, clean, and in proportion to the body, of medium length and slightly arched at the crest, setting well into the shoulders.

Topline: Appears level at a natural four-square stance.

Loin: Strong and broad when viewed from the top.

Croup: Moderately sloping.

Body: Firm and muscular.

Chest: Deep and strong.

Ribs: Well sprung.

Bottom line: Carries well back with a moderate tuck-up.

Further reading:

Structure In Action - The Makings of a Durable Dog. Pat Hastings with Wendy E. Wallace, DVM cVA and Erin Rouse. Winner of the DWAA Maxwell Award for 2011, Animal League America Award.

An Eye For a Dog: Illustrated Guide to Judging Purebred Dogs. Robert W. Cole, international conformation judge, illustrator, and author of several books and dozens of articles on purebred dogs.

Like THIS

JOHN ASHBEY PHOTOGRAPHY

Like THIS

ELISABETH EKNES PHOTOGRAPHY

MAS

AKC and FCI

The overall structure gives an impression of depth and strength without bulkiness.

Neck: Firm, clean, and in proportion to the body. It is of medium length and slightly arched at the crest, fitting well into the shoulders.

Topline: Back is firm and level from the withers to the hip joint when standing or moving.

Loin: Strong and broad when viewed from the top.

Croup: Moderately sloped.

Body: Firm and well conditioned.

Chest and Ribs: Chest is full and deep, reaching to the elbow with well-sprung ribs.

Underline: Shows a moderate tuck-up.

Topline

A dog's topline plays an important role in allowing the dog to perform the tasks for which it was bred. The topline includes the **back** (between withers and loin), the **loin** (from end of the rib cage to the hip joint) and **croup**. A strong, evenly muscled topline will give the dog endurance at a steady pace, and the loin provides spinal flexibility, enabling him to turn quickly.

When a correctly angulated and well-conditioned Aussie or MAS is trotting, his topline will appear as a smooth, level line that looks like it is floating around the ring.

Note: Handlers may stack a dog to elongate his stance, similar to the Doberman at right, in order to hide or minimize conformation faults or because it is fashionable to do so. This is NOT correct for Aussies and MAS.

Back, chest, and ribs

The back needs to be strong so it can properly support the ribcage and lungs. Aussies and MAS should have a long rib cage and sufficient depth of chest to provide maximum lung capacity for endurance. Their chests should be wide enough for sufficient lung capacity but not so wide as to interfere with gait.

LEVEL BACK and four-square stance is correct for Aussies and MAS.

A SLOPING TOPLINE is NOT correct for Aussies and MAS.

FOREQUARTERS - AUSSIES

AKC and FCI

Shoulder blades are long, flat, fairly close set at the withers and well laid back. The upper arm, which should be relatively the same length as the shoulder blade, attaches at an approximate right angle to the shoulder line. Forelegs drop straight, perpendicular to the ground.

ASCA

Shoulder blades (scapula) are well laid back, with the upper arm (humerus) slightly longer than the shoulder blade. Both the upper arm and shoulder blade are well muscled. The point of the elbow is set under the withers and is equidistant from the withers to the ground. Forelegs are straight and strong, perpendicular to the ground, with moderate bone.

FOREQUARTERS - MAS

AKC

Forequarters: The forequarters are well conditioned and balanced with the hindquarters.

Shoulders: Shoulder blades (scapula) are long, flat, fairly close set at the withers, and well laid back. The upper arm (humerus) is equal in length to the shoulder blade and meets the shoulder blade at an approximate right angle. Forelegs drop straight and perpendicular to the ground.

FCI

General appearance: The forequarters are well conditioned and balanced with the hindquarters.

Shoulder: Shoulder blades (scapula) are long, flat, fairly close set at the withers, and well laid back. The upper arm (humerus) is equal in length to the shoulder blade and meets the shoulder blade at an approximate right angle. Forelegs drop straight and perpendicular to the ground.

Elbow joint: Equidistant from the ground to the withers. Viewed from the side, the elbow should be directly under the withers. The elbows should be close to the ribs without looseness.

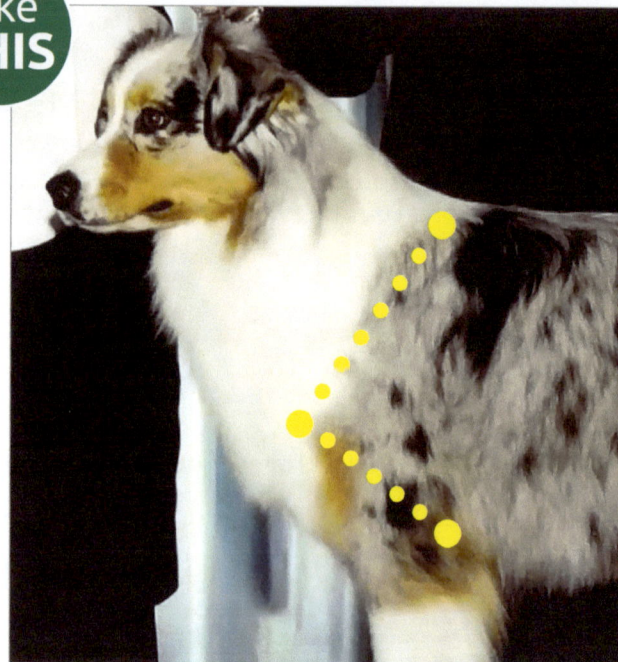

Upper arm is approximately equal in length to the shoulder blade and the bones meet at an approximate right angle.

Upper arm is shorter than the shoulder blade and the bones do not meet at a right angle, which is correct for this breed but not for Aussies and MAS.

HINDQUARTERS - AUSSIES

AKC and FCI

General appearance: The width of the hindquarters is equal to the width of the forequarters at the shoulders. The angulation of the pelvis and upper thigh corresponds to the angulation of the shoulder-blade and upper arm, forming an approximate right angle.

Stifle: Clearly defined.

Hock joints: Moderately bent. Hocks are short, perpendicular to the ground and parallel to each other when viewed from the rear.

ASCA

Width of hindquarters is approximately equal to the width of the forequarters at the shoulder. The angulation of the pelvis and upper thigh (femur) corresponds to the angulation of the shoulder blade and upper arm. The upper and lower thigh are well muscled.

Stifles: Clearly defined.

Hock joints: Moderately bent. The metatarsi are short, perpendicular
to the ground, and parallel to each other when viewed from the rear.

HINDQUARTERS - MAS

AKC and FCI

Width of hindquarters is approximately equal to the width of the forequarters at the shoulders. The angulation of the pelvis and upper thigh (femur) mirrors the angulation of the shoulder blade and upper arm, forming an approximate right angle.

Stifle: Clearly defined.

Hock: Short, perpendicular to the ground and parallel to each other when viewed from the rear.

FCI also includes:

Thigh is well muscled, but not overly so.

Hock joint: Short, moderately bent to allow the metatarsal to fall perpendicular to the ground.

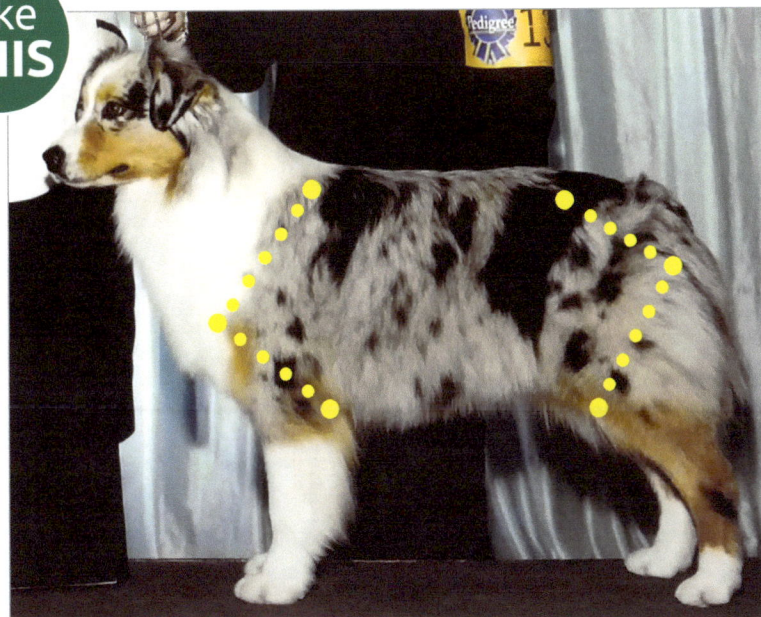

Like **THIS**

Rear angulation mirrors front angulation. Dog is in balance.

Not **THAT**

Angulation is not correctly balanced for Aussies and MAS.

AUSSIES

AKC and FCI
Stifles are clearly defined.
Hock joints moderately bent.

ASCA
Stifles are clearly defined.
Hock joints moderately bent.

MAS

AKC
Stifles are clearly defined.

FCI
Stifle (knee): stifles are clearly defined.
Hock joint: the hocks are short, moderately bent.

More is not better

Correct angulation is the amount that enables a dog to do the job for which it was originally developed.

Too much angulation reduces the ability to stop quickly and turn sharply.

Too little angulation causes an inefficient, choppy stride. Both too little and too much angulation reduce endurance.

Like **THIS**

MARCO ROSETTI PHOTOGRAPHY

CORRECT

This dog has moderate angulation of the hindquarters and correct length of bones between knee and hock joints, *as shown by the dotted yellow line.*

When viewed from the side, with the hocks forming a right angle to the ground, the correct angles and correct length of bones place his rear feet directly **underneath** the bones he sits on, *as shown by the solid yellow line.* This structure:

- provides greater accuracy of rear foot placement.
- gives the best combination of speed, endurance, and maneuverability.

This dog is able to accelerate rapidly, stop instantly, and change direction and gait swiftly, which are essential breed traits.

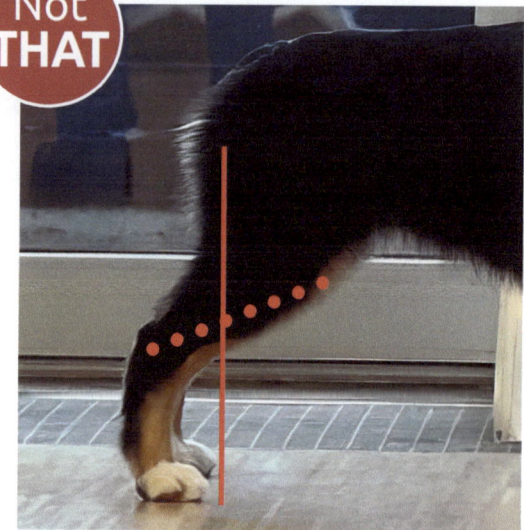

Not **THAT**

INCORRECT

This dog has excess angulation of the hindquarters, and the bones between his knee and hock joints are too long, *as shown by the dotted red line.*

When viewed from the side, with the hocks forming a right angle to the ground, the excess angles and excess length of bones cause his rear feet to be placed far out **behind** the bones he sits on, *as shown by the solid red line.* This structure:

- enables a longer trotting stride, however, it:
- reduces stamina, stability, and the ability to stop quickly and turn sharply.
- requires greater muscular strength and coordination to stabilize the hindquarters.

Any potential advantage in trotting ability is offset by muscular instability.

AUSSIES

AKC and FCI

Legs: Straight and strong. Bone is strong, oval rather than round.

Pastern: Medium length and very slightly sloped.

Front feet: Oval, compact, close knit, well-arched toes. Pads thick and resilient.

Front dewclaws: May be removed.

Hind feet: Oval, compact, close knit, well arched toes. Pads thick and resilient.

AKC ADDS: Rear dewclaws must be removed. **FCI:** No rear dewclaws.

ASCA

Forelegs: Straight and strong, perpendicular to the ground, moderate bone.

Pasterns: Short, thick, and strong, but still flexible, showing a slight angle when viewed from the side.

Front feet: Oval shaped, compact, with close knit, well-arched toes. Pads are thick and resilient; nails short and strong.

Front dewclaws: May be removed.

Hind feet: Oval shaped, compact, with close-knit, well-arched toes. Pads are thick and resilient; nails short and strong.

Rear dewclaws are removed.

MAS

AKC and FCI

Legs: Straight and strong. The bone is oval rather than round.

Pasterns: Short, thick and strong, but still flexible, showing a slight angle when viewed from the side.

Front feet: Oval shaped, compact, with close-knit, well-arched toes. Pads are thick and resilient; nails are short and strong. The nails may be any colour combination.

Front dewclaws: Should be removed (except where it is forbidden by law).

Hind feet: Oval, compact, with close knit, well arched toes. Pads are thick and resilient; nails are short and strong. The nails may be any colour combination.

AKC ADDS: Rear dewclaws should be removed. **FCI:** Rear dewclaws should be removed (in countries where it is not forbidden by law).

Aussies and MAS must have sound feet to accomplish their tasks.

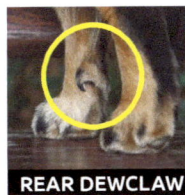

REAR DEWCLAW — JULIA BETTENDORF PHOTO

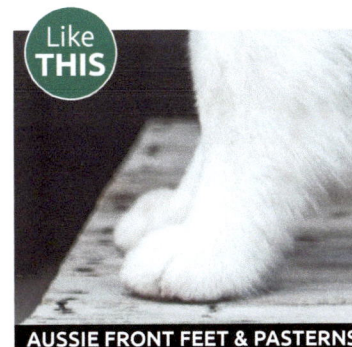

Like THIS — AUSSIE FRONT FEET & PASTERNS — ELISABETH EKNESS PHOTOGRAPHY

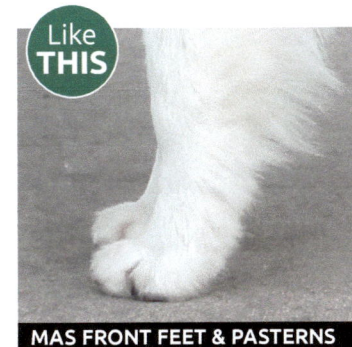

Like THIS — MAS FRONT FEET & PASTERNS — DAVE BIRREN PHOTO

DEFINITION: OVAL FEET. The two center toes are somewhat longer than the outer and inner toes. The toes on the hind feet are slightly longer than the toes on the front feet.

Like THIS — AUSSIE HIND FEET & PASTERNS — ELISABETH EKNESS PHOTOGRAPHY

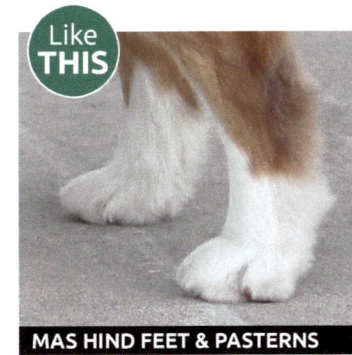

Like THIS — MAS HIND FEET & PASTERNS — DAVE BIRREN PHOTO

Not THAT — KIMBERLY DAEMERS

FAULT: Thin heel pads and/or loose ligaments can cause a dog to roll back on his heels and his front toes to tip upward. Thin pads reduce the foot's ability to absorb impact and can lead to lameness.

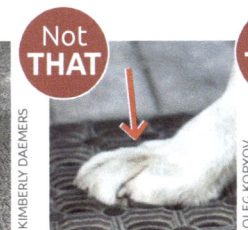

Not THAT — OLEG KOPYOV

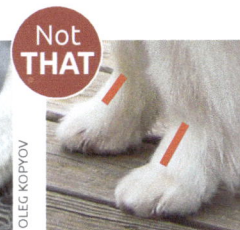

Not THAT — PAULA MCDERMID

FAULT: Flat feet and excessive slope of pasterns can lead to early lameness in dogs who engage in canine sports and other strenuous activities.

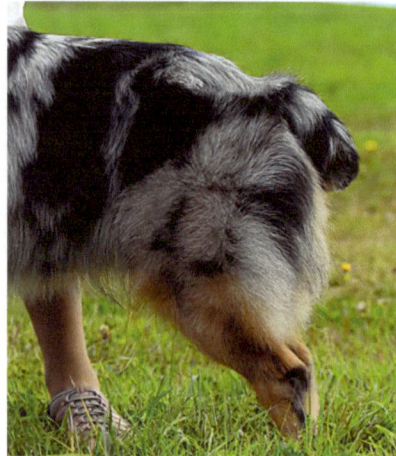

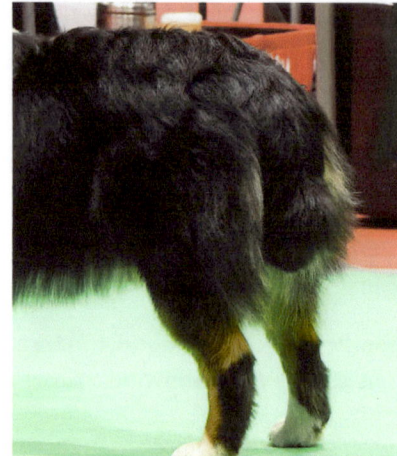

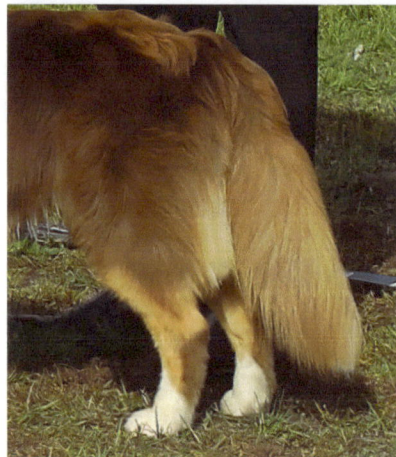

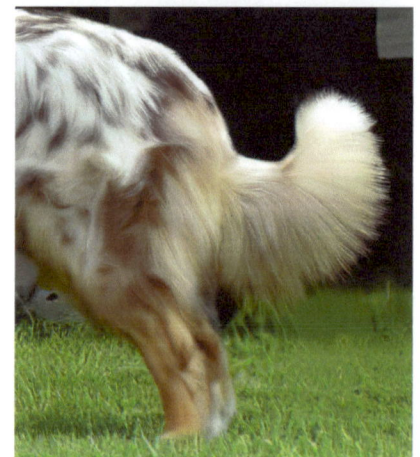

AUSSIES

AKC: Tail is straight, docked or naturally bobbed, not to exceed four inches in length.

FCI: Tail is straight, naturally long or naturally short. When docked (in countries where this practice is not forbidden), or naturally short, not to exceed 10 cm (4 inches).

ASCA: The tail is straight, not to exceed four (4) inches, natural bobtail or docked.

MAS

AKC: A docked or natural bobtail is preferred. A docked tail is straight, not to exceed three (3) inches.

FCI: A docked or natural bobtail is preferred. A docked tail is straight, not to exceed three (3) inches (in countries where docking is not forbidden by law).

AUSSIES

AKC, FCI and ASCA: Standards do not address tail carriage.

MAS

AKC and FCI: The undocked tail when at rest may hang in a slight curve. When excited or in motion the tail may be carried raised with the curve accentuated.

MONIQUE GAUTREAUX PHOTOGRAPHY

Movement
Balanced and Effortless

KAREN DELONG PHOTOGRAPHY

GÜNTER NAFFIEN PHOTO

MICHAEL ENGLISH PHOTOGRAPHY

LAS ROCOSA PHOTO

COWEN IMPRESSIONS

Correct, balanced movement. Notice how the dog's front legs and rear legs open the same distance from the midline, indicated by the yellow lines. This is balance.

JULIA BETTENDORF PHOTOGRAPHY

The rear paw lands in the footprint of the front paw. Feet skim the ground with no excess or wasted motion.

S.F. PHOTOGRAPHY

AUSSIES

AKC and FCI: The Australian Shepherd has a smooth, free and easy gait. He exhibits great agility of movement with a well-balanced, ground covering stride. The Australian Shepherd must be agile and able to change direction or alter gait instantly.

ASCA: Smooth, free, and easy, exhibiting agility of movement with a well-balanced natural stride. When viewed from the side the trot is effortless, exhibiting facility of movement rather than a hard driving action. **Exaggerated reach and drive at the trot are not desirable**.

MAS

AKC and FCI: Smooth, free, and easy; exhibiting agility of movement with a well-balanced, ground-covering stride. When traveling at a trot the head is carried in a natural position with neck extended forward and head nearly level or slightly above the topline. He must be agile and able to turn direction or alter gait instantly.

Movement is balanced and effortless. Front reach and rear drive are equal.

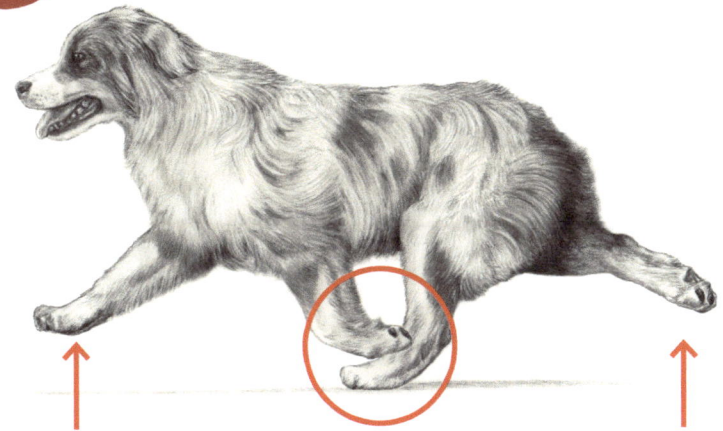

Not THAT

Exaggerated reach and drive. Extended legs lift too high off the ground. Underneath, the dog's feet interfere with each other.

This movement can be eye-catching in the show ring, but it is exhausting for a dog who needs to work all day. It reduces his ability to stop quickly and turn sharply, which is required in the breed standards.

Note: A structurally correct dog can be forced to move incorrectly by trotting him too fast. Illustration: Ian Skinner Art

Like THIS

HELENE NILSEN PHOTOGRAPHY

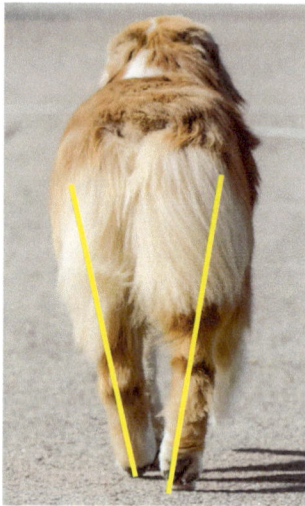

HELENE NILSEN PHOTOGRAPHY

CONNIE DUNCAN PHOTO. HART II'S SHORTY BRED BY NORMA HART

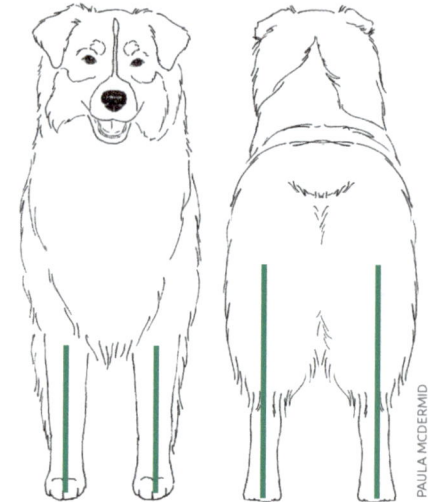

PAULA MCDERMID

AUSSIES

AKC and FCI: Fore- and hind legs move straight and parallel with the center line of the body. As speed increases, the feet (front and rear) converge toward the center line of gravity of the dog while the back remains firm and level.

ASCA: As speed increases, both front and rear feet converge equally toward the centerline of gravity beneath the body. The top line remains firm and level.

MAS

AKC and FCI: Fore- and hind legs move straight and parallel with the center line of the body; as speed increases, the feet, both front and rear, converge toward the center line of gravity of the dog, while the back remains firm and level.

Correct Movement

- Legs move in a straight column of support from the shoulders and hips to the feet.

- As speed increases, the feet converge toward the center line of gravity, resembling a "V" shape, to minimize rolling from side to side (photos 1 and 2).

- When viewed from the front, as the dog moves, the front leg on one side of the body hides the rear leg on the same side because the dog's spine is straight with the line of travel (photo 1).

- Correct structure enables the dog to move with powerful, efficient reach and drive.

Correct Stance

Front and rear legs drop straight and perpendicular to the ground.

Chest should be wide enough for sufficient lung capacity, but not so wide as to interfere with gait.

Hocks are short and parallel to each other when viewed from the rear. For greatest strength and stability, the hind legs should appear as two straight columns of support that are parallel to each other and set just slightly outside the hip sockets.

Incorrect Movement

Dogs naturally attempt to move forward with the least amount of effort, so anything that detracts from efficient movement is considered a **FAULT**. This is especially important for dogs who work hard all day. Dogs who have faulty structure and inefficient movement become exhausted and are not able to perform necessary tasks.

The trotting gait reveals the faults and virtues of a dog's conformation. Poor structure diminishes the efficiency and power of the gait and increases stress on the ligaments and tendons that support joints, which can result in pain and injury.

This page shows common movement faults that are evaluated when the dog is trotting towards and away from the judge. Incorrect movement of the legs exposes structural deficiencies of the front and rear assemblies, weak tendons and ligaments, and unstable joint conformation.

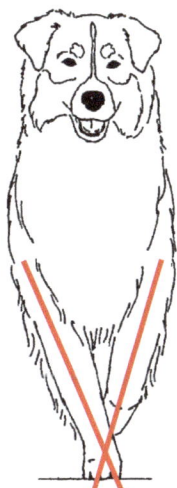
CROSSING OVER

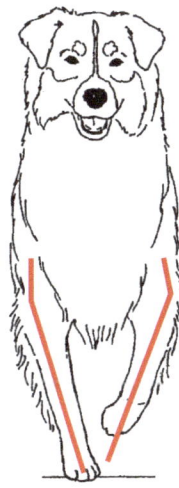
OUT AT ELBOWS

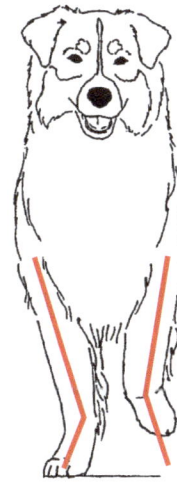
PADDLING

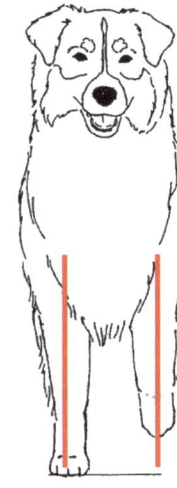
PARALLEL TRACKING

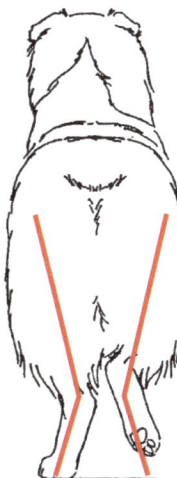
COW HOCKED

MOVING CLOSE

BOWHOCKED

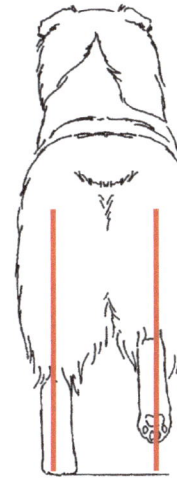
PARALLEL TRACKING

PAULA MCDERMID

Free and easy movement of a well-balanced dog.

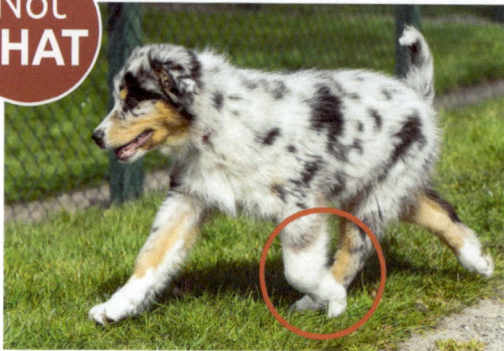

More rear angulation than front angulation. This puppy must twist his hind quarters to the side to avoid stepping on his front feet.

More front angulation than rear angulation. The physical strain from an unbalanced gait shows clearly in this dog's posture.

Balanced Angulation

- **Balanced angulation** allows thrust from the rear quarters to be transmitted smoothly and without loss of power through the back to the forequarters.

- **Balanced angulation** (front and rear angles mirror each other) facilitates good foot-timing.

- **Balanced angulation** creates a smooth, efficient, ground-covering stride which is necessary for a dog to do his job with less fatigue.

Further reading:
Dogsteps: A New Look, 3rd Edition. Definitive Manual to Canine Movement, Dog Anatomy, and Natural Gaits of Purebred Dogs; for Breeders, Judges, and Anyone Wanting to Show Dogs. Rachel Page Elliot.

Out of Balance

More rear angulation than front angulation. Over-angulated rear quarters generate excess thrust that overpowers less-angulated forequarters. The hind foot reaches beyond the front foot, causing interference. To avoid stepping on his own feet, the dog learns to twist his rear quarters to the side and move at an angle to the line of travel. This is called "crabbing," and it stresses the spine, hip joints, stifles, and hocks.

When a straighter shoulder prevents the front leg from reaching far enough forward to absorb the thrust from the rear, the front foot flips up and hits the ground too early in the stride and the leg "pounds" into the ground; the shock is absorbed by the front assembly. This jarring motion is called "pounding." Some dogs try to avoid pounding by bending their elbows and lifting their legs in a hackney motion. These types of movement strain the joints and are uncomfortable and tiring for the dog.

More front angulation than rear angulation. When shoulder angulation is greater than rear angulation, the dog won't be able to maintain a solid topline, he will fall heavily on the forehand, and he won't be able to maintain an even, flowing gait.

Unbalanced angulation is exhausting for the dog. He will not be able to endure long days of moving stock or performing other strenuous work or sports.

Correct, balanced construction provides the greatest potential for a dog to enjoy an active, healthy life.

ELISABETH EKNES PHOTOGRAPHY

Coat
Moderate and Easy Care

Hair of medium texture, straight to wavy, weather-resistant, and of medium length.

- The undercoat varies in quantity with variations in climate.
- Hair is short and smooth on the head, ears, front of forelegs, and below the hocks.
- Backs of forelegs and breeches are moderately feathered.
- There is a moderate mane and frill, more pronounced in dogs than in bitches.

AUSSIES

FCI: Hair: Of medium texture, straight to wavy, weather resistant and of medium length. The undercoat varies in quantity with variations in climate. Hair is short and smooth on the head, ears, front of forelegs and below the hocks. Backs of forelegs and breeches are moderately feathered. There is a moderate mane and frill, more pronounced in dogs than in bitches.
SEVERE FAULT: Non-typical coats.

ASCA: Coat: The coat is of medium length and texture, straight to slightly wavy, and weather resistant. The undercoat varies in quantity with climate. Hair is short and smooth on the head, outside of ears, front of forelegs, and below the hocks. Backs of forelegs are moderately feathered and breeches are moderately full. There is a moderate mane, more pronounced in dogs than bitches.
SEVERE FAULT: Non-typical coats such as excessively long; overabundant/profuse; wiry; or curly.

MAS

Coat: Moderation is the overall impression of the coat. Hair is of medium texture, straight to wavy, weather resistant, and of medium length. The undercoat varies in quantity with variations in climate. Hair is short and smooth on the head and front of the legs. The backs of forelegs and breeches are moderately feathered. There is a moderate mane and frill, more pronounced in dogs than in bitches. Hair may be trimmed on the ears, feet, back of hocks, pasterns, and tail, otherwise he is to be shown in a natural coat. Untrimmed whiskers are preferred.
SEVERE FAULT: Non-typical coats.

AMBER JADE AANENSEN PHOTOGRAPHY

AMBER JADE AANENSEN PHOTOGRAPHY

JUDIT KORÓZS-PAPP PHOTO

Excessively long

Overabundant, profuse

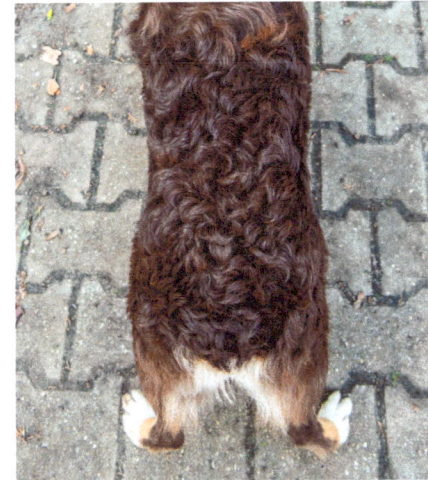

DORIEN VOGE, AAR PHOTOGRAPHY

Wiry or curly

ASCA: Non-typical coats such as excessively long; over-abundant/profuse; wiry; or curly.

Non-typical coats are SEVERE FAULTS in both breeds.

Coats should be serviceable and low-maintenance.

Aussies and MAS were developed to work livestock on all terrain and in all weather conditions. Their coats should protect them from the elements, be low maintenance, and be self-cleaning: after getting wet and/or dirty, a correct coat dries rapidly and the dirt literally falls off.

Undercoat: The undercoat is insulation, it helps keep the dog cooler in summer and warmer in winter. Aussies and MAS shed lightly all year, but more heavily in spring and fall. Dogs typically lose their winter undercoat in spring, when it is replaced by a shorter, lighter one for summer. In the fall, this cycle is reversed. Females may also shed during or after their season, and during or after a pregnancy. Dogs may also lose hair in response to stress, skin conditions, or allergies.

Mane, frill, and feathering: Less coat collects less mud and dirt and is easier to maintain.

WHY are non-typical coats undesirable?

- Excessively long coats collect more rain, snow, dirt, mud, and debris than a practical, tight-fitting coat.

- Profuse, soft textured coats are not self-cleaning and require more maintenance.

- Twigs, burrs and stickers are more difficult to remove from overabundant and curly coats.

- Excess coat can cause a dog to overheat during strenuous activity.

- Ranchers and farmers have little time to groom their dogs, so a low-maintenance coat is essential.

COURTNEY HUTHER PHOTOGRAPHY

Colours
Gorgeous Variety

Like
THIS

Black

NOËLLE HOORNEMAN PHOTOGRAPHY

Blue Merle

ELISABETH EKNES PHOTOGRAPHY

Red / Liver

SASCHA VADAGNIN PHOTOGRAPHY

Red Merle

DIANNE PHELPS PHOTOGRAPHY

AUSSIES

AKC and FCI: Colour: Blue merle, black, red merle, red—all with or without white markings and/or tan (copper) points, with no order of preference.

ASCA: Colour: All colours are strong, clear and rich. The recognized colours are blue merle, red (liver) merle, solid black, and solid red (liver), all with or without white markings and/or tan (copper) points with no order of preference.

MAS

AKC and FCI: Colour: The colouring offers variety and individuality. With no order of preference, the recognized colours are black, blue merle, red (liver), and red merle. The merle will exhibit in any amount, marbling, flecks or blotches. Undercoats may be somewhat lighter in colour than the topcoat. Asymmetrical markings are not to be faulted.

BLACK TRICOLOUR

BLACK TRICOLOUR

SOLID BLACK

BLACK & WHITE BICOLOUR

BLACK & WHITE BICOLOUR

BLACK & TAN BICOLOUR

Colour can be black with white markings and tan points (black tri-colour), solid black, black with white markings (black bi-colour), or black with tan points (black bi-colour). There is no order of preference.

LIGHT BLUE MERLE TRICOLOUR

MEDIUM BLUE MERLE TRICOLOUR

DARK BLUE MERLE TRICOLOUR

MINIMAL BLUE MERLE BICOLOUR

HEAVILY MERLED BLUE BICOLOUR

STEEL GRAY BLUE BICOLOUR

Colours range from light blue to dark steel gray with any amount of marbling, flecks, or blotches. They may have white markings and/or tan points. There is no order of preference. It is characteristic that blue merle dogs darken with age.

RED TRICOLOUR

RED TRICOLOUR

RED TRICOLOUR

RED TRICOLOUR

RED & TAN BICOLOUR

LIVER & WHITE BICOLOUR

Colour can be red with white markings and tan points (red tri-colour), solid red, red with white markings (red bi-colour), or red with tan points (red bi-colour). There is no order of preference.

RED MERLE TRICOLOUR

PHOTO COURTESY OF ISABELLE GUILLOT

LIVER RED MERLE TRICOLOUR

ELISABETH EKNES PHOTOGRAPHY

HEAVILY MERLED RED TRICOLOUR

PAULA MCDERMID PHOTO

RED MERLE TRICOLOUR

DOMINIQUE KRUWINNUS

RED MERLE & WHITE BICOLOUR

MICHAL PEVNY PHOTO

RED MERLE & WHITE BICOLOUR

CYNTHIA MONTAGUE PHOTO

Colours range from deep liver to cinnamon red with any amount of marbling, flecks, or blotches. They may have white markings and/or tan points. There is no order of preference.

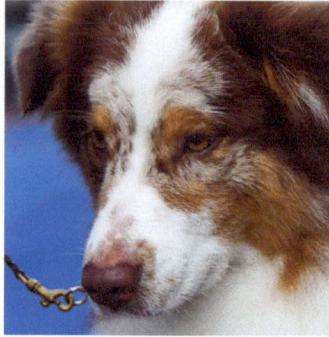

DIANA FALCONER PHOTOGRAPHY

HOLLY REGINA PRESS PHOTOGRAPHY

DEBBY MICHIELSEN PHOTO

Minimal merling

This colouring is correct.

These two dogs have very little merling and could be mistaken as solid colour when they are actually merles. The only merling on the red dog above is on her face. The rest of her body is solid red. She is genetically a red merle and can produce merle offspring if crossed with a solid colour dog.

The puppy has a black body with merling only on his face, throat, and chest. He is genetically a blue merle and has the potential to produce offspring with more common merling patterns.

This minimal merling pattern is sometimes incorrectly called cryptic or phantom merle.

WOJTECKI PHOTO

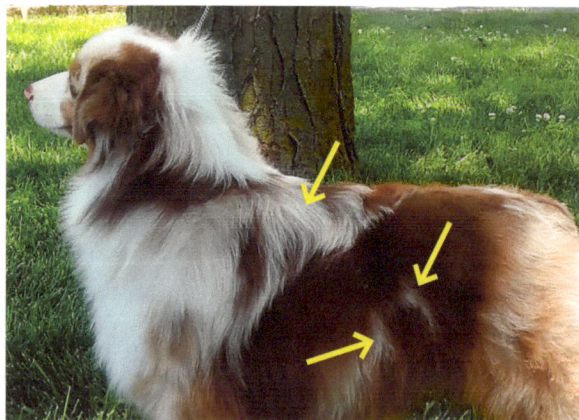

BRANDI CAREY PHOTO

Three areas of merling, not white.

Light colour merling

This colouring is correct.

Merling can be very light in colour, appearing almost white. There may be small patches of merling on the body that look similar to white body splashes, which is a disqualification.

If there is doubt, slide a white piece of paper under the gray hair to compare it to true white. Be very careful not to mistake pale gray hair for white hair, especially under artificial lighting.

Unevenly distributed merling

This colouring is correct.

The two dogs above have unevenly distributed merling patches, which is correct and equally as desirable as a coat with more evenly distributed merling patches. These breeds offer a wide variety of merling patterns and there is **no order of preference** for the amount of marbling, flecks, or blotches.

Dilution spots on merles are NOT genetically the same as dilute colour.

See page 69.

Dilution spots are isolated off-colour areas in an otherwise normally-coloured merle coat. They can be small or can cover large areas.

On blue merles, dilution spots can be shades of rusty brown or dusty gray. A rusty brown dilution spot does not mean a blue merle dog is red factored (carries the red gene), which is a common misconception.

On red merles, dilution spots are intermediate shades of red/liver.

Some of the dogs pictured on this page may be tweed or harlequin patterned merles, a trait that can be inherited independently from the merle gene.

There is probably a degree of inheritance of dilution spots, so this trait should be considered when choosing breeding pairs.

Dilution spots are cosmetic and do not affect a dog's ability to do his job, nor do they have any negative effects on his health, but **they are a deviation from the ideal.**

Dilution spot over the hip on a red merle.

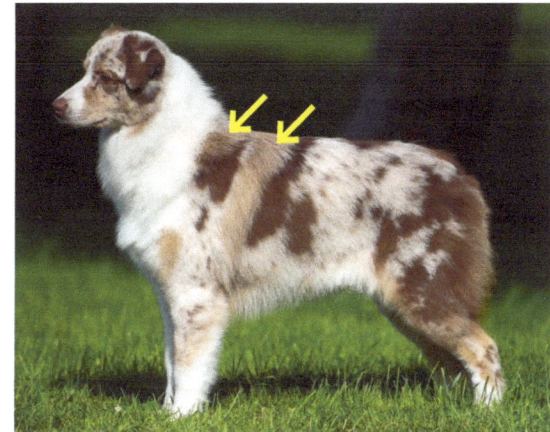

Several shades of dilution spots on a red merle.

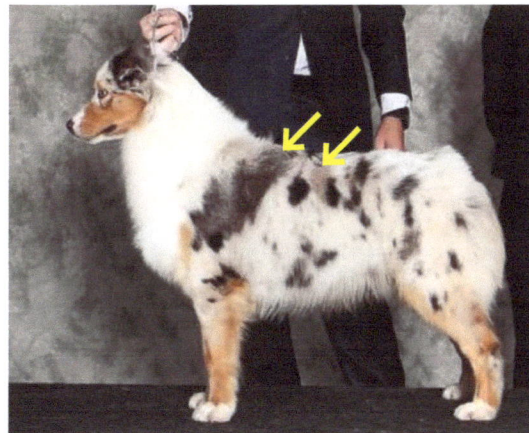

Several shades of dilution spots on a blue merle.

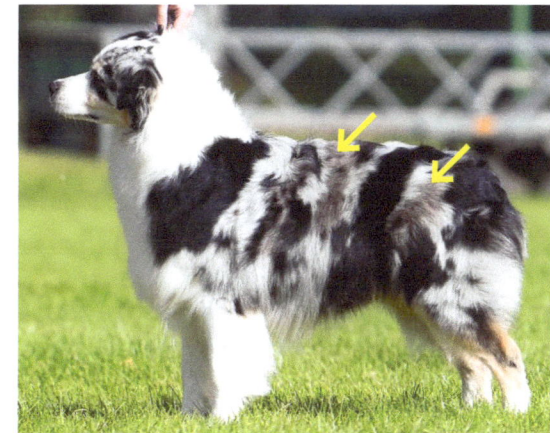

Gray-brown dilution spots on a blue merle.

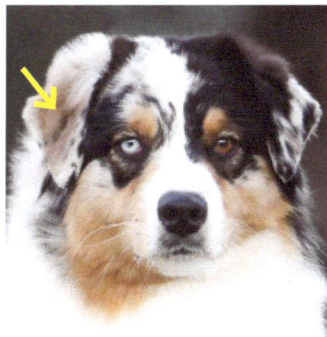

Rusty brown dilution spot on ear of blue merle.

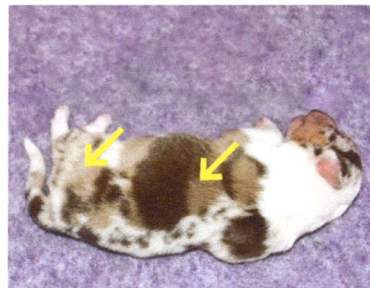

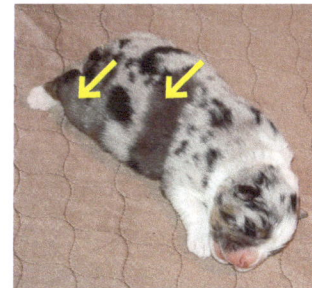

The coats of both puppies have several shades of dilution spots.

AUSSIES

AKC, FCI, ASCA: Colour: Blue merle, black, red merle, red—all with or without white markings and/or tan (copper) points.

MAS

AKC and FCI: Tan markings are not required but when present are acceptable in any or all of the following areas: around the eyes, on the feet, legs, chest, muzzle, underside of neck, face, underside of ear, underline of body, under the base of the tail and the breeches. Tan markings vary in shades from creamy beige to dark rust, with no preference. Blending with the base colour or merle pattern may be present on the face, legs, feet, and breeches.

Top row: Dogs with crisply defined tan or copper points have genes that cause the pigment to be restricted to the cheeks, muzzle, above the eyes, throat, chest, on legs, and under tail.

Middle row: Other gene combinations can fully or partially mask the tan, or blend merling into the tan areas.

Bottom row: Tan or copper points can be modified by a gene that causes the tan to spread around the eyes and onto the thighs or can extend the copper hair over more of the body.

Genetic tests can verify some genes that determine the dog's copper pattern, but many modifying genes have not yet been identified.

The images on this page show variations of tan/copper trim. All are acceptable with no order of preference.

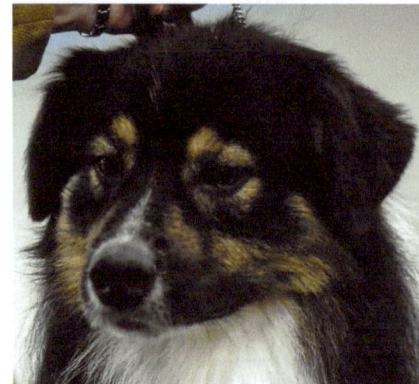

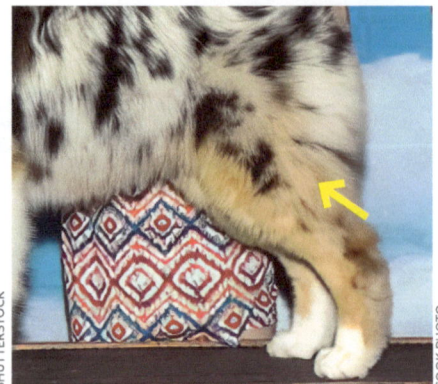

LEENA KOIVUNEN PHOTOGRAPHY

PETER LINDSAY PHOTO

THORNAPPLE PHOTO

ANN SHOPE PHOTO

SHUTTERSTOCK

COOK PHOTO

Dilute Black

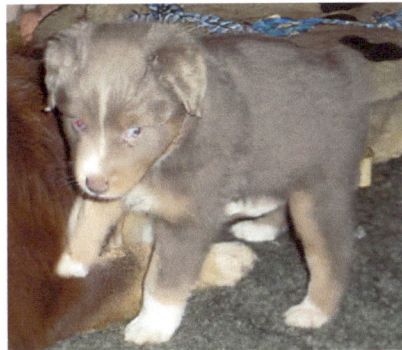

Dilute Red

Yellow

Sable

AUSSIES

AKC and FCI: FAULT
ASCA: DISQUALIFICATION: Other than recognized colours

MAS

AKC and FCI: DISQUALIFICATION: Other than recognized colours

DILUTE BLACK and **DILUTE RED** coats (which are NOT the same as dilution spots, see previous page) are the most common non-standard colour in Aussies and MAS, and are caused by the recessive MLPH gene.

- The dilution gene causes a black coat to become slate gray and the dog's nose will be slate or dark gray.
- Dilute red resembles the dusky pink colour of a Weimaraner and the nose will be light liver colour or somewhat darker.
- Dilution affects only the areas of the coat that would have been black or red/liver. Tan/copper points are not affected and are the same intensity of colour as on a non-dilute dog.
- This type of dilute colour is **not** linked with any health issues.

YELLOW dogs vary in shade from pale yellow to mahogany red and can easily be mistaken for normal red. Genetically yellow dogs are often Palomino-coloured; the hair shaft is the same colour from skin to hair tip.

- If they genetically carry tan/copper points, those are not visible.
- A genetically yellow dog with a reddish coat colour and a liver nose can be difficult to differentiate from a true red dog without genetic testing.
- Yellows may carry a merle gene which is not expressed in the coat.

SABLE dogs have reddish hair shafts that can be tipped in black or tipped in liver. There can be varying amounts of darker shading over the base coat colour.

- Dogs with black-tipped hair shafts will have black noses. Dogs with red-tipped hair shafts will have liver noses and can appear to be a normal red dog.
- Sables may carry a merle gene which is not expressed in the coat.

WHY are non-standard colours faulted or disqualified?

Non-standard colours detract significantly from breed character and may indicate mongrelization.

Yellow and **sable** can mask the presence of the merle gene. If a person didn't realize their yellow or sable dog carried a merle gene and they bred it to a typical merle, some of the offspring could be blind or deaf because they would have two copies of the merle gene.

DNA tests are available to determine genotype for some, but not all, non-typical colours.

Like THIS

AUSSIES: White spots or patches inside this area are a DISQUALIFICATION

KAROLINA SADLON-SZOT PHOTOGRAPHY

This Aussie's white collar and stifle white are well within the breed standards' descriptions. He has very little belly white.

MAS: Conspicuous, isolated spot or patch of white inside this area is a DISQUALIFICATION

ASHBEY PHOTO

This MAS's white collar, stifle white, and belly white are well within the breed standards' descriptions.

AUSSIES: Maximum acceptable belly white.
MAS: FAULT. Exceeds 1 inch (2.5 cm) above the elbow.

White coming up from the underpart (belly and stifle white)

If a dog appears to have excess white coming up from the underpart, lift up the hair to verify the location of the **root** of the hair. The root of the hair must not extend into the body colour.

AUSSIES

AKC and FCI: White is acceptable on the neck (either in part or as a full collar), chest, legs, muzzle underparts, blaze on head and white extension from underpart up to four inches (10 cm), measuring from a horizontal line at the elbow. The hairline of a white collar does not exceed the withers at the skin.

ASCA: The hairline of a white collar does not exceed the point at the withers.

MAS

AKC and FCI: White markings may be in any combination and are restricted to: the muzzle, cheeks, crown, blaze on head, the neck in a partial or full collar, chest, belly, front legs, hind legs up the hock and may extend in a thin outline of the stifle. A small amount of white extending from the underline may be visible from the side, not to exceed one inch (2.5 cm) above the elbow. The hairline of a white collar does not exceed the withers at the skin.

Note: Look at both sides of the dog because markings can be different.

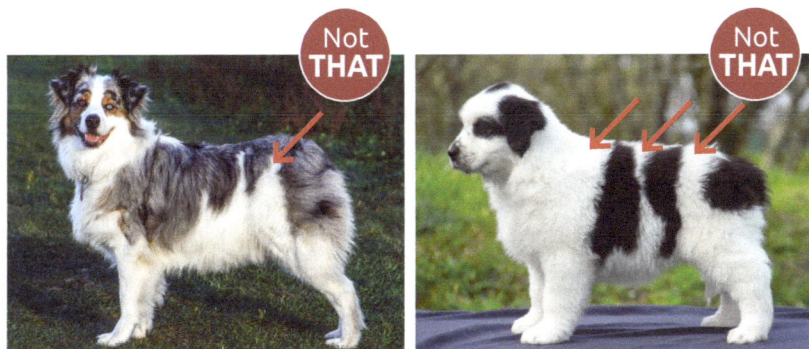

Excess Body White: Fault

AUSSIES AND MAS: FAULTED according to the degree of deviation from the ideal.

White Body Splash: Disqualification

AUSSIES AND MAS: DISQUALIFICATION: Isolated white body splash.

WHY are white body splashes disqualified and excess body and head white undesirable?

White outside of the areas described in the standards is a warning sign that there may be health problems related to lack of pigment. Excess white can be produced by several gene combinations.

- Puppies from a **merle to merle cross** that have excess white markings are frequently blind and fully or partially deaf.

- Puppies from a **solid to merle cross** that have excess white markings may have two copies of the Piebald or other white spotting genes that can be associated with deafness, particularly if there is white around the base of the ear.

DEFINITION of white body splash

AUSSIES

AKC and FCI: White body splashes, which means white on body between withers and tail, on sides between elbows and back of hindquarters in all colours. (The AKC Glossary defines "splashed" as irregularly patched, colour on white or white on colour.)

ASCA: Not defined.

MAS

AKC and FCI: White body splashes, which means any conspicuous, isolated spot or patch of white on the area between withers and tail, on back, or sides between elbows and back of hindquarters.

The white collar and white on the chest and front legs are within the breed standards.

A white collar that exceeds the point of the withers is FAULTED according to the degree of deviation from the ideal.

ALL STANDARDS

The hairline of a white collar does not exceed the point of the withers at the skin.

Hands-on examination

If the white collar of a dog appears to extend past the point of the withers, it is important to examine the collar with your hands. Lift up the hair and verify the location of the **root** of the hair. The root of the white collar hair should not exceed the point of the withers. A hands-on exam reveals that the white collar of the dog at upper left does not exceed the point of the withers and is acceptable according to the standards.

The white collar on the dog at lower left exceeds the point of the withers and she has excess white on her loin. The excess white is FAULTED according to the degree of deviation from the ideal.

When making breeding decisions, avoid pairing sires and dams who both have maximum white trim. These pairings may produce puppies with excess white trim and the possibility of deafness.

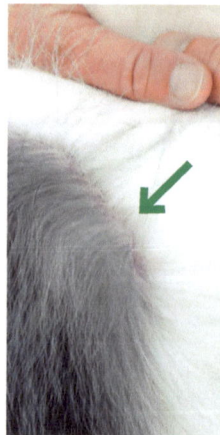

Lift up the hair of the white collar to verify the location of the root of the hair. The root should not exceed the point of the withers.

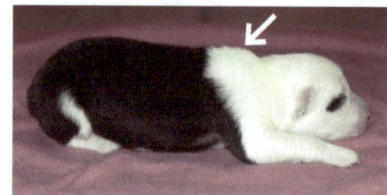

White collar exceeds point of withers.

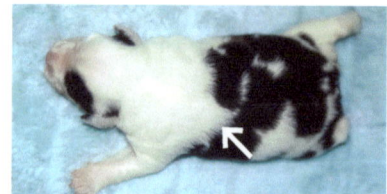

White collar exceeds point of withers.

Excess white puppies

White markings outside the areas defined in the breed standards are a warning sign that puppies may have vision and/or hearing impairments related to lack of pigment.

- Puppies from a **merle to merle cross** that have excess white markings are frequently blind and may be fully or partially deaf.

- Puppies from a **solid to merle cross** that have excess white markings may have two copies of the Piebald or other white spotting genes that can be associated with deafness, particularly if there is white around the base of the ear.

White on ears

AUSSIES

AKC and FCI: White on the head should not predominate.

ASCA: On all colours the areas surrounding the ears and eyes are dominated by colour other than white.

MAS

AKC and FCI: Ears fully covered by colour are preferred. **AKC: SEVERE FAULT:** White markings covering over 25 percent of an ear.

WHY?

White surrounding the ears can predispose dogs to deafness. If the hair cells in the inner ear lack pigment, the nerve endings will atrophy and die in the first few weeks of life and full or partial deafness will result. However, many dogs with white ears have normal hearing. If in doubt, consult a professional.

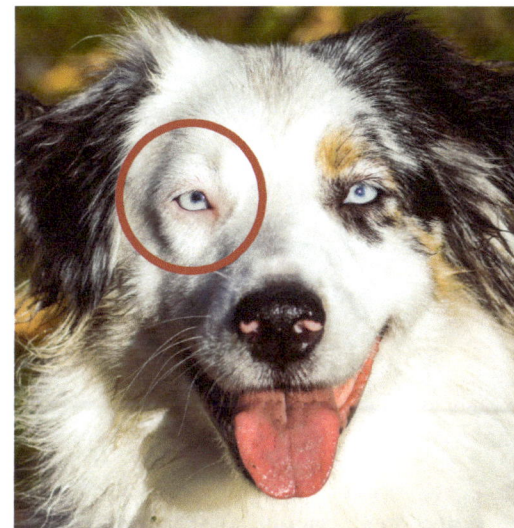

White should not surround eyes

AUSSIES

AKC and FCI: White on the head should not predominate, and the eyes must be fully surrounded by colour and pigment.

ASCA: On all colours the areas surrounding the ears and eyes are dominated by colour other than white.

MAS

AKC and FCI: White on the head does not predominate, and the eyes are fully surrounded by colour and pigment.

WHY?

White colour around the eyes may indicate eye defects resulting from improper development of the tissues of the eye. This applies only to puppies from **merle to merle** pairings.

AUSSIES	MAS
White markings **AKC and FCI:** White is acceptable on the neck (either in part or as a full collar), chest, legs, muzzle underparts, blaze on head and white extension from underpart up to four inches, measuring from a horizontal line at the elbow. **ASCA:** With or without white markings.	**White markings** **AKC and FCI:** White Markings: White markings are not required but when present do not dominate. Ticking may be present in white markings. White markings may be in any combination and are restricted to: the muzzle, cheeks, crown, blaze on head, the neck in a partial or full collar, chest, belly, front legs, hind legs up the hock and may extend in a thin outline of the stifle. If a natural undocked tail is present, the tip of the tail may have white.
White on head **AKC and FCI:** White on the head should not predominate, and the eyes must be fully surrounded by colour and pigment. **ASCA:** On all colours the areas surrounding the ears and eyes are dominated by colour other than white.	**White on head** **AKC and FCI:** White on the head does not predominate, and the eyes are fully surrounded by colour and pigment. Ears fully covered by colour are preferred. **AKC: Severe Fault:** White markings covering over 25 percent of an ear.
White collar **AKC and FCI:** The hairline of a white collar does not exceed the point of the withers at the skin. **ASCA:** The hairline of a white collar does not exceed the point at the withers.	**White collar** **AKC and FCI:** The hairline of a white collar does not exceed the withers at the skin.
White belly extension **AKC and FCI:** White extension from underpart up to 4 inches (10 cm), measuring from a horizontal line at the elbow. **ASCA:** Not described.	**White belly extension** **AKC and FCI:** A small amount of white extending from the underline may be visible from the side, not to exceed one inch (2.5 cm) above the elbow.
Disqualification **AKC and FCI:** White body splashes, which means [isolated] white on body between withers and tail, on sides between elbows and back of hindquarters in all colours. **ASCA:** White body splashes (not defined).	**Disqualification** **AKC and FCI:** White body splashes, which means any conspicuous, isolated spot or patch of white on the area between withers and tail, on back, or sides between elbows and back of hindquarters.

Not THAT

Faults
Severe Faults
Disqualifications

FAULTS are deviations from the standards that interfere with the dog's ability to perform its original purpose. If a feature or quality is desirable it should only be present in the right measure.

AUSSIES

FCI: Any departure from the foregoing points should be considered a **FAULT** and the seriousness with which the fault should be regarded should be in exact proportion to its degree and its effect upon the health and welfare of the dog.

ASCA:

FAULT: A level bite. Missing teeth should be faulted to the degree that they deviate from a full complement of 42 teeth.

FAULT: Any deviation from almond-shaped eyes.

GAIT FAULTS shall be penalized according to the degree of deviation from the ideal.

MAS

FCI: Any departure from the foregoing points should be considered a **FAULT** and the seriousness with which the fault should be regarded should be in exact proportion to its degree and its effect upon the health and welfare of the dog and its ability to perform its traditional work.

AKC and FCI: FAULT: Noses that are less than fully pigmented.

SEVERE FAULT: EARS

AUSSIES

AKC and FCI: Prick ears and hanging ears.

ASCA: Prick ears; overly large ears; low set ears with no lift from the base.

MAS

AKC and FCI: Prick ears and ears that hang with no lift.

SEVERE FAULT: COAT

AUSSIES

AKC and FCI: Non-typical coats.

ASCA: Non-typical coats such as excessively long; overabundant/profuse; wiry; or curly.

MAS

AKC and FCI: Non-typical coats.

SEVERE FAULT: NOSE PIGMENT

AUSSIES

AKC and FCI: More than 25% unpigmented nose on dogs over 1 year of age.

MAS

AKC and FCI: 25% to 50% unpigmented nose leather.

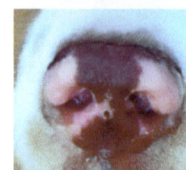

SEVERE FAULT: WHITE ON EARS

MAS

AKC: White markings covering over 25% of an ear.

SEVERE FAULT: TEMPERAMENT

AUSSIES

AKC: Any display of shyness, fear or aggression.

DISQUALIFICATION: SIZE

MAS

AKC and FCI: Under 14 inches (35.5 cm) and over 18 inches (46 cm) for dogs; under 13 inches (33 cm) and over 17 inches (43.5 cm) for bitches. Minimum heights do not apply to dogs or bitches under 6 months old.

DISQUALIFICATION: NOSE PIGMENT

AUSSIES

ASCA: Dudley nose (a pink nose with no dark pigment).

MAS

AKC and FCI: Over 50% unpigmented nose leather.

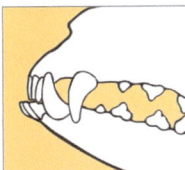

DISQUALIFICATION: BITE

AUSSIES

AKC and FCI: Undershot. Overshot greater than 1/8 inch. Loss of contact caused by short center incisors in an otherwise correct bite shall not be judged undershot.

ASCA: Undershot bite, overshot bite, wry mouth. Teeth broken or missing by accident shall not be penalized.

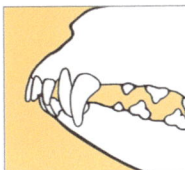

MAS

AKC and FCI: Undershot or overshot bite. Teeth broken or missing by accident shall not be penalized.

DISQUALIFICATION: TEMPERAMENT

AUSSIES and MAS

FCI: Aggressive or overly shy.

DISQUALIFICATION: WHITE BODY SPLASH

AUSSIES

AKC and FCI: White body splashes, which means [isolated] white on body between withers and tail, on sides between elbows and back of hindquarters in all colours.

ASCA: White body splashes.

MAS

AKC and FCI: White body splashes, which means any conspicuous, isolated spot or patch of white on the area between withers and tail, on back, or sides between elbows and back of hindquarters.

DISQUALIFICATION: COLOUR

Dilute Black, Dilute Red, Yellow, Sable

AUSSIES

ASCA: Other than recognized colours.

MAS

AKC and FCI: Other than recognized colours.

DISQUALIFICATION: ABNORMALITIES

Monorchidism and cryptorchidism: One or both testicles did not descend into the scrotum.
Any dog clearly showing physical or behavioral abnormalities.

PAULA MCDERMID

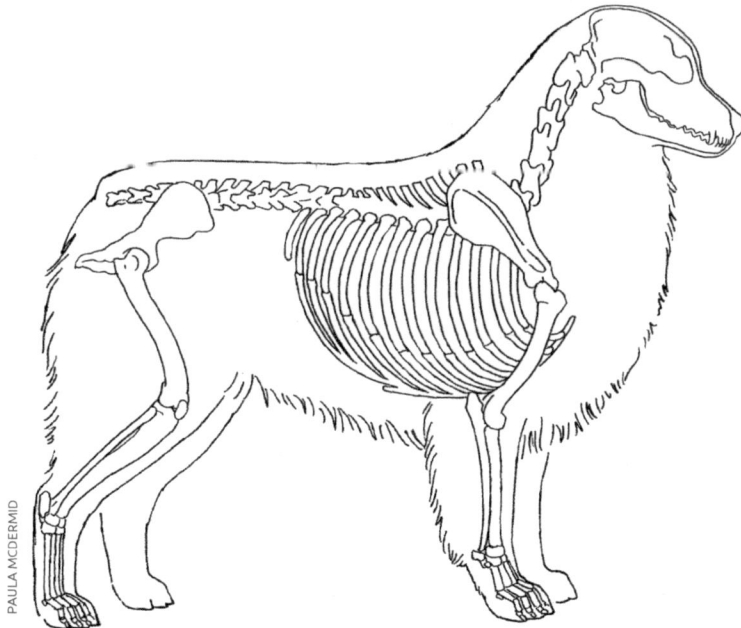

Breed Standards

General Appearance:

The Australian Shepherd is an intelligent working dog of strong herding and guarding instincts. He is a loyal companion and has the stamina to work all day. He is well balanced, slightly longer than tall, of medium size and bone, with colouring that offers variety and individuality. He is attentive and animated, lithe and agile, solid and muscular without cloddiness. He has a coat of moderate length and coarseness. He has a docked or natural bobbed tail.

Size, Proportion, Substance:

SIZE: The preferred height for males is 20 to 23 inches, females 18 to 21 inches. Quality is not to be sacrificed in favor of size.

PROPORTION: Measuring from the breastbone to rear of thigh and from top of the withers to the ground the Australian Shepherd is slightly longer than tall.

SUBSTANCE: Solidly built with moderate bone. Structure in the male reflects masculinity without coarseness. Bitches appear feminine without being slight of bone.

Head:

THE HEAD is clean cut, strong and dry. Overall size should be in proportion to the body. The muzzle is equal in length or slightly shorter than the back skull. Viewed from the side the topline of the back skull and muzzle form parallel planes, divided by a moderate, well-defined stop. The muzzle tapers little from base to nose and is rounded at the tip.

EXPRESSION: Showing attentiveness and intelligence, alert and eager. Gaze should be keen but friendly.

EYES are brown, blue, amber or any variation or combination thereof, including flecks and marbling. Almond shaped, not protruding nor sunken. The blue merles and blacks have black pigmentation on eye rims. The red merles and reds have liver (brown) pigmentation on eye rims.

EARS are triangular, of moderate size and leather, set high on the head. At full attention they break forward and over, or to the side as a rose ear. Prick ears and hanging ears are severe faults.

SKULL: Top flat to slightly domed. It may show a slight occipital protuberance. Length and width are equal. Moderate well-defined stop.

MUZZLE tapers little from base to nose and is rounded at the tip.

NOSE: Blue merles and blacks have black pigmentation on the nose (and lips). Red merles and reds have liver (brown) pigmentation on the nose (and lips). On the merles it is permissible to have small pink spots; however, they should not exceed 25 percent of the nose on dogs over one year of age, which is a **SERIOUS FAULT.**

TEETH: A full complement of strong white teeth should meet in a scissors bite or may meet in a level bite.

DISQUALIFICATIONS: Undershot. Overshot greater than ⅛ inch. Loss of contact caused by short center incisors in an otherwise correct bite shall not be judged undershot. Teeth broken or missing by accident shall not be penalized.

Neck, Topline, Body:

NECK is strong, of moderate length, slightly arched at the crest, fitting well into the shoulders.

TOPLINE: Back is straight and strong, level and firm from withers to hip joints. The croup is moderately sloped.

BODY: Chest is not broad but is deep with the lowest point reaching the elbow. The ribs are well sprung and long, neither barrel chested nor slab-sided. The underline shows a moderate tuck-up. Tail is straight, docked or naturally bobbed, not to exceed four inches in length.

Forequarters:

SHOULDERS: Shoulder blades are long, flat, fairly close set at the withers and well laid back. The upper arm, which should be relatively the same length as the shoulder blade, attaches at an approximate right angle to the shoulder line with forelegs dropping straight, perpendicular to the ground. Legs straight and strong.

BONE is strong, oval rather than round. Pastern is medium length and very slightly sloped. Front dewclaws may be removed.

FEET are oval, compact with close knit, well arched toes. Pads are thick and resilient.

Hindquarters:

The width of the hindquarters is equal to the width of the forequarters at the shoulders. The angulation of the pelvis and upper thigh corresponds to the angulation of the shoulder blade and upper arm, forming an approximate right angle.

STIFLES are clearly defined, hock joints moderately bent.

HOCKS are short, perpendicular to the ground and parallel to each other when viewed from the rear.

REAR dewclaws must be removed.

FEET are oval, compact with close knit, well arched toes. Pads are thick and resilient.

Coat:

HAIR is of medium texture, straight to wavy, weather resistant and of medium length. The undercoat varies in quantity with variations in climate. Hair is short and smooth on the head, ears, front of forelegs and below the hocks. Backs of forelegs and britches are moderately feathered. There is a moderate mane and frill, more pronounced in dogs than in bitches.

Non-typical coats are **SEVERE FAULTS.**

Colour:

BLUE merle, black, red merle, red-all with or without white markings and/or tan (copper) points, with no order of preference.

THE HAIRLINE of a white collar does not exceed the point of the withers at the skin.

WHITE is acceptable on the neck (either in part or as a full collar), chest, legs, muzzle underparts, blaze on head and white extension from underpart up to four inches, measuring from a horizontal line at the elbow. White on the head should not predominate, and the eyes must be fully surrounded by colour and pigment. Merles characteristically become darker with increasing age.

COLOUR DISQUALIFICATION: White body splashes, which means white on body between withers and tail, on sides between elbows and back of hindquarters in all colours.

Gait:

The Australian Shepherd has a smooth, free and easy gait. He exhibits great agility of movement with a well-balanced, ground covering stride. Fore and hind legs move straight and parallel with the center line of the body. As speed increases, the feet (front and rear) converge toward the center line of gravity of the dog while the back remains firm and level. The Australian Shepherd must be agile and able to change direction or alter gait instantly.

Temperament:

The Australian Shepherd is an intelligent, active dog with an even disposition; he is good natured, seldom quarrelsome. He may be somewhat reserved in initial meetings.

SEVERE FAULT: Any display of shyness, fear or aggression is to be severely penalized.

Disqualifications:

*   Undershot. Overshot greater than 1/8 inch.

*   White body splashes, which means white on body between withers and tail, on sides between elbows and back of hindquarters in all colours.

Approved May 14, 1991
Effective January 1, 1993

ORIGIN: U.S.A.

DATE OF PUBLICATION OF THE OFFICIAL VALID STANDARD: 26.03.2009.

UTILIZATION: Farm and ranch shepherd dog.

CLASSIFICATION F.C.I.: Group 1 Sheepdogs and Cattle dogs (except Swiss Cattle dogs) Section 1 Sheepdogs without working trial

Brief Historical Summary:

While there are many theories as to the origin of the Australian Shepherd, the breed as we know it today developed exclusively in the United States. The Australian Shepherd was given its name because of the association with Basque Sheepherders who came to the United States from Australia in the 1800's.

The Australian Shepherd's popularity rose steadily with the boom of western horseback riding after World War II, which became known to the general public via rodeos, horse shows, movies, and television shows. Their inherent versatile and trainable personality made them assets to American farms and ranches. The American stockman continued the development of the breed, maintaining its versatility, keen intelligence, strong herding instincts, and eye-catching appearance that originally won their admiration.

Although each individual is unique in colour and markings, all Australian Shepherds show an unsurpassed devotion to their families. Their many attributes have guaranteed the Australian Shepherd's continued popularity.

General Appearance:

The Australian Shepherd is well balanced, slightly longer than tall, of medium size and bone, with colouring that offers variety and individuality.

He is attentive and animated, lithe and agile, solid and muscular without cloddiness. He has a coat of moderate length and coarseness. He has a docked or natural tail.

Important Proportions:

Measuring from the breastbone to rear of thigh and from top of the withers to the ground the Australian Shepherd is slightly longer than tall.

Solidly built with moderate bone. Structure in the male reflects masculinity without coarseness. Bitches appear feminine without being slight of bone.

Behaviour/Temperament:

The Australian Shepherd is an intelligent working dog of strong herding and guarding instincts. He is a loyal companion and has the stamina to work all day. With an even disposition, he is good natured, seldom quarrelsome. He may be somewhat reserved in initial meetings.

Head:

THE HEAD is clean cut, strong and dry. Overall size should be in proportion to the body.

CRANIAL REGION: SKULL: Top flat to slightly domed. It may show a slight occipital protuberance. Length and width are equal.

STOP: Moderate, well-defined.

Facial Region:

NOSE: Blue merles and blacks have black pigmentation on the nose (and lips). Red merles and reds have liver (brown) pigmentation on the nose (and lips). On the merles it is permissible to have small pink spots; however, they should not exceed 25 % of the nose on dogs over one year of age, which is a **SERIOUS FAULT.**

MUZZLE: Equal in length or slightly shorter than the back skull. Viewed from the side the topline of the back skull and muzzle form parallel planes, divided by a moderate, well-defined stop. The muzzle tapers little from base to nose and is rounded at the tip.

JAWS/TEETH: A full complement of strong white teeth should meet in a scissors bite or may meet in a pincer bite.

EYES: Brown, blue, amber or any variation or combination thereof, including flecks and marbling. Almond shaped, not protruding nor sunken. The blue merles and blacks have black pigmentation on eye rims. The red merles and reds have liver (brown) pigmentation on eye rims.

EXPRESSION: Showing attentiveness and intelligence, alert and eager. Gaze should be keen but friendly.

EARS: Triangular, of moderate size and leather, set high on the head. At full attention they break forward and over, or to the side as a rose ear.

NECK: Strong, of moderate length, slightly arched at the crest, fitting well into the shoulders.

Body:

TOP LINE: Back straight and strong, level and firm from withers to hip joints.

CROUP: Moderately sloping.

CHEST: Not broad, but deep with the lowest point reaching the elbow. Ribs: Well sprung and long, neither barrel chested nor slab-sided.

UNDERLINE AND BELLY: Shows a moderate tuck-up.

TAIL: Straight, naturally long or naturally short. When docked (in countries where this practice is not forbidden), or naturally short, not to exceed 10 cm.

Limbs - Forequarters:

SHOULDER: Shoulder-blades long, flat, fairly close set at the withers and well laid back. The upper arm, which should be relatively the same length as the shoulder-blade, attaches at an approximate right angle to the shoulder line with forelegs dropping straight, perpendicular to the ground.

LEGS: Straight and strong. Bone strong, oval rather than round.

METACARPUS (Pastern): Medium length and very slightly sloping. Front dewclaws may be removed.

FOREFEET: Oval, compact, with close-knit, well-arched toes. Pads thick and resilient.

Hindquarters:

GENERAL APPEARANCE: The width of the hindquarters is equal to the width of the forequarters at the shoulders.

ANGULATION of the pelvis and upper thigh corresponds to the angulation of the shoulder-blade and upper arm, forming an approximate right angle

STIFLE: Clearly defined.

HOCK JOINTS: Moderately bent. Hocks: Short, perpendicular to the ground and parallel to each other when viewed from the rear. No rear dewclaws.

HIND FEET: Oval, compact with close-knit, well-arched toes. Pads thick and resilient.

Gait:

The Australian Shepherd has a smooth, free and easy gait. He exhibits great agility of movement with a well-balanced, ground covering stride. Fore-and hind legs move straight and parallel with the centre line of the body. As speed increases, the feet (front and rear) converge toward the centre line of gravity of the dog while the back remains firm and level. The Australian Shepherd must be agile and able to change direction or alter gait instantly.

Coat:

HAIR: Of medium texture, straight to wavy, weather resistant and of medium length. The undercoat varies in quantity with variations in climate. Hair is short and smooth on the head, ears, front of forelegs and below the hocks. Backs of forelegs and breeches are moderately feathered. There is a moderate mane and frill, more pronounced in dogs than in bitches.

COLOUR: Blue merle, black, red merle, red – all with or without white markings and/or tan markings, with no order of preference.

HAIRLINE of a white collar does not exceed the point of the withers at the skin.

WHITE is acceptable on the neck (either in part or as a full collar), chest, legs, muzzle underparts, blaze on head and white extension from underpart up to four inches (10 cm), measuring from a horizontal line at the elbow. White on the head should not predominate, and the eyes must be fully surrounded by colour and pigment. Merles characteristically become darker with increasing age.

Size:

HEIGHT at the withers: The preferred height for males is 20-23 inches (51-58 cm), females 18-21 inches (46-53 cm). Quality is not to be sacrificed in favour of size.

Faults:

- Any departure from the foregoing points should be considered a fault and the seriousness with which the fault should be regarded should be in exact proportion to its degree and its effect upon the health and welfare of the dog.

Severe Faults:

- Prick ears and hanging ears.

- Non-typical coats.

Disqualifying Faults:

- Aggressive or overly shy.

- Any dog clearly showing physical of behavioural abnormalities.

- Undershot. Overshot by more than 1/8 inch. Loss of contact caused by short center incisors in an otherwise correct bite shall not be judged undershot. Teeth broken or missing by accident shall not be penalized.

- White body splashes in all colours, which means white on body between withers and tail, on sides between elbows and back of hindquarters.

N.B. (*Nota Bene:* please note)

- Male animals should have two apparently normal testicles fully descended into the scrotum.

- Only functionally and clinically healthy dogs, with breed typical conformation, should be used for breeding.

VIRGINIA FLEMING PHOTO

SUSAN LAWLEY SEVERNS PHOTOGRAPHY

BECKY PARKER / DALLY UP PHOTOGRAPHY

PAULA MCDERMID PHOTO

DORIEN VOGELAAR PHOTOGRAPHY

Introduction:

First and foremost, the Australian Shepherd is a true working stockdog, and anything that detracts from his usefulness as such is undesirable. The most important breed characteristics are overall moderation in size and bone, balance with correct proportions, and sound movement

General Appearance:

The Australian Shepherd is a well-balanced dog of medium size and bone. He is attentive and animated, showing strength and stamina combined with unusual agility. Slightly longer than tall, he has a coat of moderate length and coarseness with colouring that offers variety and individuality in each specimen. An identifying characteristic is his natural or docked bobtail. In each sex, masculinity or femininity is well defined.

Character:

The Australian Shepherd is primarily a working dog of strong herding and guardian instincts. He is an intelligent, exceptional companion. He is versatile and easily trained: performing his assigned tasks with great style and enthusiasm. He is reserved with strangers but does not exhibit shyness. This unusually versatile stockdog works with the power and quickness to control difficult cattle as well as the ability to move sheep without unnecessary roughness. Although an aggressive, authoritative worker, viciousness toward people or animals is intolerable.

Head:

The **HEAD** is clean-cut, strong, dry, and in proportion to the body.

The **TOPSKULL** is flat to slightly rounded; its length and width each equal to the length of the muzzle.

The **MUZZLE** is of medium width and depth and tapers gradually to a rounded tip, without appearing heavy or snipey.

LIPS are close fitting, meeting at the mouthline.

The **TOPLINES OF THE MUZZLE AND TOPSKULL** appear close to parallel.

The **STOP** is moderate but well defined.

(A) TEETH: A full complement of strong white teeth meet in a scissors bite. **A LEVEL BITE IS A FAULT.** Teeth broken or missing by accident are not penalized. All other missing teeth should be faulted to the degree that they deviate from a full complement of 42 teeth.

DISQUALIFICATIONS: Undershot bite, Overshot bite, Wry Mouth

(B) EYES: The eyes are very expressive, showing attentiveness and intelligence. They are clear, almond-shaped, of moderate size, and set a little obliquely, neither prominent nor sunken. The pupils are dark, well defined, and perfectly positioned.

EYE COLOUR is brown, blue, amber; or any variation or combination, including flecks and marbling. All eye colours are acceptable in combination with all coat colours.

FAULTS: Any deviation from almond-shaped eyes.

(C) EARS: The ears are set high on the side of the head, are triangular, of moderate size and slightly rounded at the tip. The tip of the ear reaches to, but not further than, the inside corner of the nearest eye. At full attention, the ears should lift from one-quarter (¼) to one-half (½) above the base and break forward or slightly to the side.

SEVERE FAULTS: Prick ears; overly large ears; low set ears with no lift from the base.

Neck And Body:

The **NECK** is firm, clean, and in proportion to the body. It is of medium length and slightly arched at the crest, setting well into the shoulders.

The **BODY** is firm and muscular.

The **TOPLINE** appears level at a natural four-square stance.

The **BOTTOM LINE** carries well back with a moderate tuck-up.

The **CHEST** is deep and strong with ribs well sprung.

The **LOIN** is strong and broad when viewed from the top.

The **CROUP** is moderately sloping.

The **TAIL** is straight, not to exceed 4 inches, natural bobtail or docked.

Forequarters:

The **SHOULDER BLADES** (scapula) are well laid back, with the upper arm (humerus) slightly longer than the shoulder blade. Both the upper arm and shoulder blade are well muscled.

The **FORELEGS** are straight and strong, perpendicular to the ground, with moderate bone.

The **POINT OF THE ELBOW** is set under the withers and is equidistant from the withers to the ground.

PASTERNS are short, thick, and strong, but still flexible, showing a slight angle when viewed from the side.

FEET are oval shaped, compact, with close knit, well-arched toes. Pads are thick and resilient; nails short and strong. Dewclaws may be removed.

Hindquarters:

WIDTH OF HINDQUARTERS is approximately equal to the width of the forequarters at the shoulder. The angulation of the pelvis and upper thigh (femur) corresponds to the angulation of the shoulder blade and upper arm. The upper and lower thigh are well muscled.

STIFLES are clearly defined; hock joints moderately bent.

The **METATARSI** are short, perpendicular to the ground, and parallel to each other when viewed from the rear.

FEET are oval shaped, compact, with close-knit, well-arched toes. Pads are thick and resilient; nails short and strong. Rear dewclaws are removed.

Coat:

The coat is of medium length and texture, straight to slightly wavy, and weather resistant. The undercoat varies in quantity with climate. Hair is short and smooth on the head, outside of ears, front of forelegs, and below the hocks. Backs of forelegs are moderately feathered and breeches are moderately full. There is a moderate mane, more pronounced in dogs than bitches. The Australian Shepherd is a working dog and is to be shown with a natural coat.

> **SEVERE FAULTS:** Non-typical coats such as excessively long; over-abundant/profuse; wiry; or curly.

Colour:

All colours are strong, clear and rich. The recognized colours are blue merle, red (liver) merle, solid black, and solid red (liver) all with or without white markings and/or tan (copper) points with no order of preference.

The blue merle and black have black pigmentation on nose, lips and eye-rims. Reds and red merles have liver pigmentation on nose, lips and eye rims.

- Butterfly nose should not be faulted under one year of age.
- On all colours the areas surrounding the ears and eyes are dominated by colour other than white.
- The hairline of a white collar does not exceed the point at the withers.

  COLOUR DISQUALIFICATIONS:

- Other than recognized colours.
- White body splashes.
- Dudley nose.

Gait:

Smooth, free, and easy, exhibiting agility of movement with a well-balanced natural stride. As speed increases, both front and rear feet converge equally toward the centerline of gravity beneath the body. The top line remains firm and level. When viewed from the side the trot is effortless, exhibiting facility of movement rather than a hard driving action. Exaggerated reach and drive at the trot are not desirable. **GAIT FAULTS** shall be penalized according to the degree of deviation from the ideal.

Size:

Preferred height at the withers for males is 20 to 23 inches; that for females is 18 to 21 inches, however, quality is not to be sacrificed in favor of size.

Other Disqualifications:

- Monorchidism and cryptorchidism.

Created January 15, 1977: Amended June 01, 2013

General Appearance:

The Miniature American Shepherd is a small size herding dog that originated in the United States. He is slightly longer than tall with bone that is moderate and in proportion to body size and height without extremes. Movement is smooth, easy, and balanced. Exceptional agility combined with strength and stamina allows for working over a variety of terrain. This highly versatile, energetic dog makes an excellent athlete with superior intelligence and a willingness to please those to whom he is devoted. He is both a loyal companion and a biddable worker, which is evident in his watchful expression. The double coat of medium length and coarseness may be solid in colour or merled, with or without white and/or tan (copper) markings. He traditionally has a docked or natural bobtail.

Size, Proportion and Substance:

SIZE: Height for dogs is 14 inches up to and including 18 inches at the top of the withers. Height for bitches is 13 inches up to and including 17 inches at the top of withers.

DISQUALIFICATION: Under 14 inches and over 18 inches for dogs; under 13 inches and over 17 inches for bitches. The minimum heights set forth in this Breed Standard shall not apply to dogs or bitches under six months of age.

PROPORTION: Measuring from the point of the shoulder to the point of the buttocks and from the highest point of the shoulder blade to the ground, he is slightly longer than tall.

SUBSTANCE: Solidly built with moderate bone in proportion to body height and size. Structure in the dog reflects masculinity without coarseness. Bitches appear feminine without being slight of bone.

Head:

The **HEAD** is clean-cut, dry, and in proportion to the body.

EXPRESSION: Alert, attentive and intelligent. May express a reserved look and/or be watchful of strangers.

EYES: The eyes are set obliquely, almond shaped, neither protruding nor sunken and in proportion to the head. Acceptable in all coat colours, one or both eyes may be brown, blue, hazel, amber or any colour combination thereof, including flecks and marbling.

The **EYE RIMS** of the reds and red merles have full red (liver) pigmentation. The eye rims of the blacks and blue merles have full black pigmentation.

EARS: Are triangular, of moderate size, set high on the head. At full attention they break forward and over, or to the side as a rose ear.

SEVERE FAULT: Prick ears and ears that hang with no lift.

Skull:

THE CROWN is flat to slightly round and may show a slight occipital protuberance. The width and the length of the crown are equal.

STOP: The stop is moderate but defined.

MUZZLE: The muzzle is of medium width and depth and tapers gradually to a rounded tip without appearing heavy, square, snipy, or loose. Length is equal to the length of the crown.

PLANES: Viewed from the side, the muzzle and the top line of the crown are slightly oblique to each other, with the front of the crown on a slight angle downward toward the nose.

NOSE: Red merles and reds have red (liver) pigmentation on the nose leather. Blue merles and blacks have black pigmentation on the nose leather. Fully pigmented noses are preferred.

NOSES that are less than fully pigmented will be **FAULTED**.

SEVERE FAULT: 25 to 50 percent unpigmented nose leather.

DISQUALIFICATION: Over 50 percent un-pigmented nose leather.

BITE: A full complement of teeth meet in a scissor bite. Teeth broken, missing or discoloured by accident are not penalized.

DISQUALIFICATION: Undershot or overshot bite.

Neck, Topline and Body:

The overall structure gives an impression of depth and strength without bulkiness.

NECK: The neck is firm, clean, and in proportion to the body. It is of medium length and slightly arched at the crest, fitting well into the shoulders.

TOPLINE: The back is firm and level from the withers to the hip joint when standing or moving.

LOIN: The loin is strong and broad when viewed from the top.

CROUP: The croup is moderately sloped.

BODY: The body is firm and well conditioned.

CHEST AND RIBS: The chest is full and deep, reaching to the elbow, with well sprung ribs.

UNDERLINE: The underline shows a moderate tuck-up.

TAIL: A docked or natural bobtail is preferred. A docked tail is straight, not to exceed three (3) inches. The undocked tail when at rest may hang in a slight curve. When excited or in motion the tail may be carried raised with the curve accentuated.

Forequarters:

The **FOREQUARTERS** are well conditioned and balanced with the hindquarters.

SHOULDERS: Shoulder blades (scapula) are long, flat, fairly close set at the withers, and well laid back.

UPPER ARM: The upper arm (humerus) is equal in length to the shoulder blade and meets the shoulder blade at an approximate right angle. The forelegs drop straight and perpendicular to the ground.

ELBOW: The elbow joint is equidistant from the ground to the withers. Viewed from the side, the elbow should be directly under the withers. The elbows should be close to the ribs without looseness.

LEGS: The legs are straight and strong. The bone is oval rather than round.

PASTERNS: Short, thick and strong, but still flexible, showing a slight angle when viewed from the side.

FEET: Oval shaped, compact, with close-knit, well-arched toes. Pads are thick and resilient; nails are short and strong. The nails may be any colour combination. Dewclaws should be removed.

Hindquarters:

WIDTH of hindquarters is approximately equal to the width of the forequarters at the shoulders.

ANGULATION: The angulation of the pelvis and upper thigh (femur) mirrors the angulation of the shoulder blade and upper arm, forming an approximate right angle.

STIFLE: Stifles are clearly defined.

HOCK: The hocks are short, perpendicular to the ground and parallel to each other when viewed from the rear.

FEET: Feet are oval, compact, with close knit, well arched toes. Pads are thick and resilient; nails are short and strong. The nails may be any colour combination. Rear dewclaws should be removed.

Coat:

Moderation is the overall impression of the coat. Hair is of medium texture, straight to wavy, weather resistant, and of medium length. The undercoat varies in quantity with variations in climate. Hair is short and smooth on the head and front of the legs. The backs of forelegs and breeches are moderately feathered. There is a moderate mane and frill, more pronounced in dogs than in bitches. Hair may be trimmed on the ears, feet, back of hocks, pasterns, and tail, otherwise he is to be shown in a natural coat. Untrimmed whiskers are preferred.

   SEVERE FAULT: Non-typical coats.

Colour:

The colouring offers variety and individuality. With no order of preference, the recognized colours are black, blue merle, red (liver) and red merle. The merle will exhibit in any amount, marbling, flecks or blotches. Undercoats may be somewhat lighter in colour than the topcoat. Asymmetrical markings are not to be faulted.

Tan Markings:

Tan markings are not required but when present are acceptable in any or all of the following areas: around the eyes, on the feet, legs, chest, muzzle, underside of neck, face, underside of ear, underline of body, under the base of the tail and the breeches. Tan markings vary in shades from creamy beige to dark rust, with no preference. Blending with the base colour or merle pattern may be present on the face, legs, feet, and breeches.

White Markings:

White markings are not required but when present do not dominate. Ticking may be present in white markings. White on the head does not predominate, and the eyes are fully surrounded by colour and pigment. Red merles and reds have red (liver) pigmentation on the eye rims. Blue merles and blacks have black pigmentation on the eye rims.

EARS fully covered by colour are preferred.

SEVERE FAULT: White markings covering over 25 percent of an ear.

WHITE MARKINGS may be in any combination and are restricted to: the muzzle, cheeks, crown, blaze on head, the neck in a partial or full collar, chest, belly, front legs, hind legs up the hock and may extend in a thin outline of the stifle. A small amount of white extending from the underline may be visible from the side, not to exceed one inch above the elbow.

The **HAIRLINE OF A WHITE COLLAR** does not exceed the withers at the skin. If a natural undocked tail is present, the tip of the tail may have white.

DISQUALIFICATIONS: Other than recognized colours. White body splashes, which means any conspicuous, isolated spot or patch of white on the area between withers and tail, on back, or sides between elbows and back of hindquarters.

Gait:

Smooth, free, and easy; exhibiting agility of movement with a well-balanced, ground-covering stride. Fore and hind legs move straight and parallel with the center line of the body; as speed increases, the feet, both front and rear, converge toward the center line of gravity of the dog, while the back remains firm and level.

When traveling at a trot the head is carried in a natural position with neck extended forward and head nearly level or slightly above the topline. He must be agile and able to turn direction or alter gait instantly.

Temperament:

The Miniature American Shepherd is intelligent, primarily a working dog of strong herding and guardian instincts. An exceptional companion, he is versatile and easily trained, performing his assigned tasks with great style and enthusiasm. Although reserved with strangers, he does not exhibit shyness. He is a resilient and persistent worker, who adjusts his demeanor and arousal appropriately to the task at hand. With his family he is protective, good natured, devoted and loyal.

Disqualifications:

- Under 14 inches and over 18 inches for dogs; under 13 inches and over 17 inches for bitches. The minimum heights set forth in this Breed Standard shall not apply to dogs or bitches under six months of age.
- Over 50 percent unpigmented nose leather.
- Undershot or overshot bite.
- Other than recognized colours.
- White body splashes, which means any conspicuous, isolated spot or patch of white on the area between withers and tail, on back, or sides between elbows and back of hindquarters.

Effective June 27, 2012

ORIGIN: United States of America.

PATRONAGE: Hungary.

DATE OF PUBLICATION OF THE OFFICIAL VALID STANDARD: 04/09/2019.

UTILIZATION: Farm and ranch shepherd dog.

FCI-CLASSIFICATION: Group 1 Sheepdogs and Cattledogs (except Swiss Cattledogs) Section 1 Sheepdogs. Without working trial.

Brief Historical Summary:

The Miniature American Shepherd was developed in California during the late 1960's with the breeding of small Australian Shepherds. These dogs were bred with a goal of maintaining their small size, active character and intelligence. The breed was first registered with the National Stock Dog Registry in 1980 and was originally called the Miniature Australian Shepherd. By the early 1990's, they had attained nationwide popularity and were shown in various rare-breed organizations. The first parent breed club and registry, MASCUSA, was formed in 1990 and incorporated in 1993. The breed entered the AKC Foundation Stock Service as the Miniature American Shepherd in May 2011. The Miniature American Shepherd Club of the USA (MASCUSA) is the designated national parent club of the American Kennel Club.

The breed has been used for herding smaller stock such as sheep and goats, although they have the heart to tackle larger stock as well. Their small size was looked upon with favor, as they could more easily double as a household pet. They became especially popular with equestrians traveling to horse shows, as their intelligence, loyalty, and size made them an excellent travel companion. In this way their popularity spread across the country.

Today, the Miniature American Shepherd is established across the U.S. and internationally. It is a breed with a unique identity - an eye catching, versatile little herding dog, equally at home on a ranch or in the city.

General Appearance:

The Miniature American Shepherd is a small size herding dog that originated in the United States. He is slightly longer than tall with bone that is moderate and in proportion to body size and height without extremes. Movement is smooth, easy, and balanced. Exceptional agility combined with strength and stamina allows for working over a variety of terrain. This highly versatile, energetic dog makes an excellent athlete with superior intelligence and a willingness to please those to whom he is devoted. He is both a loyal companion and a biddable worker, which is evident in his watchful expression. The double coat of medium length and coarseness may be solid in colour or merled, with or without white and/or tan (copper) markings. He traditionally has a docked or natural bobtail.

Important Proportions:

Measuring from the point of the shoulder to the point of the buttocks and from the highest point of the shoulder blade to the ground, he is slightly longer than tall. Substance - Solidly built with moderate bone in proportion to body height and size. Structure in the dog reflects masculinity without coarseness. bitches appear feminine without being slight of bone. The overall structure gives an impression of depth and strengt without bulkiness.

Behaviour/Temperament:

The Miniature American Shepherd is intelligent, primarily a working dog of strong herding and guardian instincts. An exceptional companion, he is versatile and easily trained, performing his assigned tasks with great style and enthusiasm. Although reserved with strangers, he does not exhibit shyness. He is a resilient and persistent worker, who adjusts his demeanor and arousal appropriately to the task at hand. With his family he is protective, good natured, devoted and loyal.

Head:

CRANIAL REGION: SKULL: The crown is flat to slightly round and may show a slight occipital protuberance. The width and the length of the crown are equal.

STOP: The stop is moderate but defined.

Facial Region:

NOSE: Red merles and reds have red (liver) pigmentation on the nose leather. Blue merles and blacks have black pigmentation on the nose leather. Fully pigmented noses are preferred.

NOSES that are less than fully pigmented will be FAULTED.

SEVERE FAULT – 25 to 50 percent unpigmented nose leather.

MUZZLE: The muzzle is of medium width and depth and tapers gradually to a rounded tip without appearing heavy, square, snipy, or loose. Length is equal to the length of the crown. Planes - Viewed from the side, the muzzle and the top line of the crown are slightly oblique to each other, with the front of the crown on a slight angle downward toward the nose

LIPS: pigment to match colour of dog, to be tight fitting.

JAWS/TEETH: A full complement of teeth meet in a scissor bite. Teeth broken, missing or discoloured by accident are not penalized.

DISQUALIFICATION - Undershot or overshot bite.

EYES: The eyes are set obliquely, almond shaped, neither protruding nor sunken and in proportion to the head. Acceptable in all coat colours, one or both eyes may be brown, blue, hazel, amber or any colour combination thereof, including flecks and marbling. The eye rims of the reds and red merles have full red (liver) pigmentation. The eye rims of the blacks and blue merles have full black pigmentation. The expression is alert, attentive, and intelligent. They may express a reserved look or be watchful of strangers.

EARS: Are triangular, of moderate size, set high on the head. At full attention they break forward and over, or to the side as a rose ear.

SEVERE FAULT - Prick ears and ears that hang with no lift.

NECK: The neck is firm, clean, and in proportion to the body. It is of medium length and slightly arched at the crest, fitting well into the shoulders.

Body:

THE BODY is firm and well-conditioned

TOP LINE: The back is firm and level from the withers to the hip joint when standing or moving.

WITHERS: Shoulder blades (scapula) are long, flat, fairly close set at the withers, and well laid back.

BACK: The back is firm and level from the withers to the hip joint when standing or moving.

LOIN: The loin is strong and broad when viewed from the top.

CROUP: The croup is moderately sloped.

CHEST: The chest is full and deep, reaching to the elbow, with well sprung ribs.

UNDERLINE AND BELLY: The underline show a moderate tuck-up.

TAIL: A docked or natural bobtail is preferred. A docked tail is straight, not to exceed three (3) inches (in countries where it is not forbidden by law). The undocked tail when at rest may hang in a slight curve. When excited or in motion the tail may be carried raised with the curve accentuated.

Limbs - Forequarters:

GENERAL APPEARANCE: The forequarters are well conditioned and balanced with the hindquarters.

FORELEGS: The forelegs drop straight and perpendicular to the ground. The legs are straight and strong. The bone is oval rather than round.

SHOULDER: Shoulder blades (scapula) are long, flat, fairly close set at the withers, and well laid back.

UPPER ARM: The upper arm (humerus) is equal in length to the shoulder blade and meets the shoulder blade at an approximate right angle.

ELBOW: The elbow joint is equidistant from the ground to the withers. Viewed from the side, the elbow should be directly under the withers. The elbows should be close to the ribs without looseness

FOREARM: The legs are straight and strong. The bone is oval rather than round.

METACARPUS (pastern): Short, thick and strong, but still flexible, showing a slight angle when viewed from the side.

FOREFEET: Oval shaped, compact, with close-knit, well-arched toes. Pads are thick and resilient; nails are short and strong. The nails may be any colour combination. Dewclaws should be removed (except where it is forbidden by law).

Hindquarters:

GENERAL APPEARANCE: Width of hindquarters is approximately equal to the width of the forequarters at the shoulders. Angulation - The angulation of the pelvis and upper thigh (femur) mirrors the angulation of the shoulder blade and upper arm, forming an approximate right angle.

THIGH: The thigh is well muscled, but not overly so.

STIFLE (knee): Stifles are clearly defined.

HOCK JOINT: The hocks are short, moderately bent to allow the metatarsal to fall perpendicular to the ground.

METATARSUS (Rear pastern): The metatarsals are short, perpendicular to the ground when viewed from the side and parallel to each other when viewed from the rear.

HIND FEET: Feet are oval, compact, with close knit, well arched toes. Pads are thick and resilient; nails are short and strong. The nails may be any colour combination. Rear dewclaws should be removed (in countries where it is not forbidden by law).

Gait / Movement:

The gait is smooth, free and easy exhibiting agility of movement with a well-balanced, ground-covering stride. The fore and hind legs move straight and parallel with the center line of the body; as speed increases, the feet, both front and rear, converge toward the center line of gravity of the dog while the back remains firm and level. When traveling at a trot, the head is carried in a natural position with the neck extended forward and head nearly level or slightly above the topline. He must be agile and able to turn direction or alter gait instantly.

Skin:

SKIN is of typical moderate thickness and laxiety.

Coat:

MODERATION is the overall impression of the coat. Hair is of medium texture, straight to wavy, weather resistant, and of medium length. The undercoat varies in quantity with variations in climate.

HAIR: Hair is short and smooth on the head and front of the legs. The backs of forelegs and breeches are moderately feathered. There is a moderate mane and frill, more pronounced in dogs than in bitches. Hair may be trimmed on the ears, feet, back of hocks, pasterns, and tail, otherwise he is to be shown in a natural coat. Untrimmed whiskers are preferred.

SEVERE FAULT: Non-typical coats.

Colour:

BODY COLOUR: The colouring offers variety and individuality. With no order of preference, the recognized colours are black, blue merle, red, liver and red or liver merle. The merle will exhibit in any amount, marbling, flecks or blotches. Undercoats may be somewhat lighter in colour than the topcoat. Asymmetrical markings are not to be faulted.

TAN MARKINGS: Tan markings are not required but when present are acceptable in any or all of the following areas: around the eyes, on the feet, legs, chest, muzzle, underside of neck, face, underside of ear, underline of body, under the base of the tail and the breeches. Tan markings vary in shades from creamy beige to dark rust, with no preference. Blending with the base colour or merle pattern may be present on the face, legs, feet, and breeches.

WHITE MARKINGS: White markings are not required but when present do not dominate. Ticking may be present in white markings. White on the head does not predominate, and the eyes are fully surrounded by colour and pigment.

Red merles and reds have red (liver) pigmentation on the eye rims. Blue merles and blacks have black pigmentation on the eye rims.

EARS fully covered by colour are preferred.

White markings may be in any combination and are restricted to the muzzle, cheeks, crown, blaze on head, the neck in a partial or full collar, chest, belly, front legs, hind legs up the hock and may extend in a thin outline of the stifle. A small amount of white extending from the underline may be visible from the side, not to exceed one inch above the elbow.

HAIRLINE of a white collar does not exceed the withers at the skin. If a natural **UNDOCKED TAIL** is present, the tip of the tail may have white.

Size and Weight:

Height at the withers:

MALES: 35.5 cm up to 46 cm at the top of the withers

FEMALES: 33 cm up to and including 43.5 cm at the top of the withers.

WEIGHT: Healthy weight will vary based on individual size, sex and substance.

Faults:

- Any departure from the foregoing points should be considered a fault and the seriousness with which the fault is regarded should be in exact proportion to its degree and its effect upon the health and welfare of the dog and its ability to perform its traditional work.

Severe Faults:

- Non-typical coats.
- Prick ears and ears that hang with no lift.
- Between 25 and 50% unpigmented nose leather
- White markings covering over 25% of an ear

Disqualifying Faults:

- Aggressive or extremely shy dogs.
- Any dog clearly showing physical or behavioral abnormalities.
- Under 35.5 cm and over 46 cm for dogs; under 33 cm and over 43.5 cm for bitches. The minimum heights set forth in this Breed Standard shall not apply to dogs or bitches under six months of age.
- Over 50 percent unpigmented nose leather.
- Undershot or overshot bite.
- Other than recognized colours.
- White body splashes, which means any conspicuous, isolated spot or patch of white on the area between withers and tail, on back, or sides between elbows and back of hindquarters.

N.B. (*Nota Bene:* please note)

- Male animals should have two apparently normal testicles fully descended into the scrotum.
- Only functionally and clinically healthy dogs, with breed typical conformation should be used for breeding.

KAREN PENCE PHOTO

MONTANA MAGIC PHOTOGRAPHY

DIANA MINGALIEVA PHOTO

Paula McDermid

Author and Designer

Australian Shepherd Club of America breeder-judge licensed in 1986. American Kennel Club breeder-judge licensed in 1995. ASCA Hall of Fame Kennel "Bainbridge" established in 1980. Breeder of Best in Specialty Show and Group winners, National Specialty Most Versatile Aussie award-winner, and nationally top-ranked Aussie in agility. Licensed to judge nine American Kennel Club breeds. Former Vice President, Health and Genetics Chairperson, and board member of the United States Australian Shepherd Association. Author of five books about Australian Shepherds.

Claudia Bosselmann

Collaborator

Breeder of Australian Shepherds since 2002 under the "Rafter Creek" kennel name. Licensed by the FCI to judge Australian Shepherds in 2012 and Miniature American Shepherds in 2019. President of the Club für Australian Shepherd Germany for 20 years; this club has also been responsible for the Miniature American Shepherd in Germany since 2019. Bred and owned FCI Worldwinner, FCI Jahrhundertsieger, VDH Bundessieger, VDH Europasieger, multiple Champions, and German Champion Obedience. Licensed by the FCI to also judge Siberian Huskies, Alaskan Malamutes, Islandic Sheepdogs, Lapinkoira, and Samoyed. Author of two books about Australian Shepherds.

Inga Cerbule

Collaborator

Imported the first Australian Shepherds to the Baltic States in 1994. Established the Australian Shepherd kennel "Sentikki" in 1998. Licensed by the FCI to judge Australian Shepherds in 2017. Licensed by the FCI to judge Miniature American Shepherds in 2019. Qualified by the FCI to judge FCI Group 1 (Herding Group). Owned or bred World Winners, European Winners, Best in Show and Group winners. Secretary of the FCI Breeding Commission, Board member of the Latvian Kennelclub (FCI). Lecturer at the Latvian University of Life Sciences, Veterinary Medicine program. Lecturer at the Latvian Kennel Club, Continuing Education Program for judges and breeders.

www.ingramcontent.com/pod-product-compliance
Lightning Source LLC
Chambersburg PA
CBHW041552030426

42336CB00004B/49